OUR EUROPEAN
NEIGHBOURS

EDITED BY
WILLIAM HARBUTT DAWSON

SPANISH LIFE IN TOWN AND
COUNTRY

Spanish Life in Town and Country

BY

L. HIGGIN

With Chapters on

Portuguese Life in Town and Country

BY

EUGENE E. STREET

PUBLISHED FOR THE

BAY VIEW READING CLUB

GENERAL OFFICE : 165 BOSTON BOULEVARD
DETROIT, MICH.

BY G. P. PUTNAM'S SONS

NEW YORK   LONDON

The Knickerbocker Press, New York

NOTE BY THE EDITOR

IT has been thought well to include Portugal in this volume, so as to embrace the entire Iberian Peninsula. Though geographically contiguous, and so closely associated in the popular mind, the Spanish and Portuguese nations offer in fact the most striking divergences alike in character and institutions, and separate treatment was essential in justice to each country. The preferential attention given to Spain is only in keeping with the more prominent part she has played, and may yet play, in the history of civilisation.

I AM indebted for the chapters on Portugal to Mr. Eugène E. Street, whose long and intimate acquaintance with the land and its people renders him peculiarly fitted to draw their picture.

L. HIGGIN.

CONTENTS

SPANISH LIFE

vii

Contents

INTRODUCTORY

SECOND AND ENLARGED EDITION

MR. HIGGIN has presented in this volume graceful and picturesque sketches showing the life of to-day in a country which during a century or more has been struggling upward out of the abyss into which it had been sunk by despotism, bigotry, and bad government. During the later years, under more enlightened rulers, many important reforms, social, educational, and administrative, have been undertaken, and wise and far-reaching plans of regeneration are in train for the furthering of the welfare of a people which, while submissive and loyal, is apathetic and ignorant. The present rulers of Spain take the ground that orderly liberty must follow, and not precede, enlightenment.

It is the misfortune of Spain that the sceptre of Charles III. passed into the hands of an amiable fool at a most critical period of modern times, when half civilisation was crazy with the new conviction that the face of society, and even the laws of nature, could be suddenly altered by changes in the form of governments. In England

this belief was modified by the stolid good sense
of the race, loyalty to the throne, and the elas-
ticity of the constitution under which we lived ;
in France it was turned to his own advantage by
one of the greatest geniuses and most unscrupu-
lous men the world ever saw, and has resulted in
a successful democracy which at intervals cries
for a despot to save it from itself; whilst in Spain,
where the throne had forfeited right to respect,
where there was no constitution to be elastic, and
no genius to rescue society from anarchy by new
developments of despotism, the people themselves
have painfully worked out, so far, their own sal-
vation at the cost of a century of conflict and
misery untold.

Again and again during the period, political
empirics have prescribed rapid remedies for a
chronic disease, always with the result that a
crisis has been provoked which has further re-
tarded the progress of the patient. False guides
have betrayed the people from the straight upward path through short cuts into quagmires, or
to the edge of the precipice ; at every level rest-
ing-place the leaders have declared loudly that
the summit has been attained, and in eloquent
orations have called upon their followers, and the
world at large, to witness and admire their cleverness in having reached it with so little labour.
Every transient gleam of their own poor rushlight
has been hailed in resounding phrases as the
bright sunshine which was to be the final goal.

The people in the meanwhile, inexperienced in the phenomena of progress, have readily taken flowing oratory for noble deeds, and flickering candles for the day's effulgence; only to give way to bitter disappointment and paroxysms of rage when they have learnt the truth, and have been forced to toil upward again still in the twilight.

But, withal, the road has led them higher. The squabbles and corruptions of politicians, the folly and blindness of those who sat in high places, have done their worst; but those who have patience to read to the end the story here told will see that in the course of the century the Spanish nation, in spite of all, has advanced, and is still advancing, though slowly, towards the material prosperity and enlightened freedom which is the right of all civilised peoples.

I may fairly claim to possess some special qualifications for relating many of the incidents set forth in this history. In my youth I have listened open-eyed for hours to the tales of aged relatives and their friends who had borne active part in the great struggle early in the century. Some of them had been friends of Godoy, some of them companions in arms of Wellington and Hill; and from the mouth of one I learnt the tragic story of the massacre of the 2d of May, at which he had been present. The same aged gentleman and his brother, near relatives of my own, were amongst the victims of the despotism of Fernando, and expiated in prison and in exile

their adhesion to the cause of the Constitution.
From them, many a time and oft, have I heard
on the spot the story of the battle of the Constitution in the Calle Mayor of Madrid on the 7th
of July, 1822, and of the storming of the palace
stairs by Diego de Leon in 1841 to capture the
young Queen Isabel. At a later period my own
observation commenced, and as a keenly interested spectator and friend of many of the chief
actors I witnessed most of the stirring scenes re-
counted in these pages, from the revolution of
1868 up to the death of Alfonso XII., since when
I have never ceased to follow closely the incidents
of the contemporary history of Spain.

In a work containing so many details, I cannot
hope to have escaped errors, but I may claim that
I have done my best to avoid them ; and I have
been careful to confirm my memory of the events
I have witnessed, and of descriptions given to me
by actors in earlier scenes, by comparison with
other contemporary accounts.

SPANISH LIFE IN TOWN AND COUNTRY

SPANISH LIFE IN TOWN AND COUNTRY

CHAPTER I

LAND AND PEOPLE

ONLY in comparatively late years has the Iberian Continent been added to the happy hunting-grounds of the ordinary British and American tourist, and somewhat of a check arose after the outbreak of the war with America. To the other wonderful legends which gather round this romantic country, and are spread abroad, unabashed and uncontradicted, was added one more, to the effect that so strong a feeling existed on the part of the populace against Americans, that it was unsafe for English-speaking visitors to travel there. Nothing is farther from the truth; there is no hatred of American or English, and, if there had been, they little know the innate courtesy of the Spanish people, who fear

insult that is not due to the overbearing manners
of the tourist himself.

To-day, however, everyone is going to Spain,
and as the number of travellers increases, so, perhaps, does the real ignorance of the country and
of her people become more apparent, for, after a
few days, or at most weeks, spent there, those who
seem to imagine that they have discovered Spain,
as Columbus discovered America, deliver their
judgment upon her with all the audacity of ignorance, or, at best, with very imperfect information and capacity for forming an opinion.

For many years, the foreign element in Spain
was so small that all who made their home in the
country were known and easily counted, while
those who travelled were, for the most part, cultivated people—artists, or lovers of art, or persons
interested in some way in the commercial or industrial progress of the nation. Even in those
days, however, too many tourists spent their time
amongst the dead cities, remnants of Spain's great
past, and came back to add their quota to the
sentimental notions current about the romantic
land sung by Byron. Wrapped in a glamour for
which their own enthusiasm was mainly responsible, they beheld all things coloured with the
rich glow of a resplendent sunset; their descriptions of people and places raised expectations too
often cruelly dispelled by facts, as presented to
those of less exuberant imaginations.

On the other hand, the mere British traveller,

knowing nothing of art, almost nothing of history, and very little of anything beyond his own provincial parish, finds all that is not the commonplace of his own country, barbarous and utterly beneath contempt. His own manners, not generally of the best, set all that is proud and dignified in the lowest Spaniard in revolt; he imagines that he meets with discourtesy where, in fact, he has gone out to seek it, and his own ignorance is chiefly to blame for his failure to understand a people wholly unlike his own class associates at home. He, too, returns, shaking the dust off his feet, to draw a picture of the land he has left, as false and misleading as that of the dreamer who has overloaded his picture with colour that does not exist for the ordinary tourist. Thus it too often comes to pass that visitors to Spain experience keen disappointment during their short stay in the country. Whether they always acknowledge it or not, is another question.

To hit the happy medium, and to draw from a tour in Spain, or from a more prolonged sojourn there, all the pleasure that may be derived from it, and to feel with those who, knowing the country and its people intimately, love it dearly, a remembrance of its past history and of its strange agglomeration of nationalities is absolutely necessary; nor can any true idea be formed of the country from a mere acquaintance with any one of its widely differing provinces. Galicia is, even to-day, more nearly allied to Portugal than to Spain, and it was only in 1668 that the independence of the former was acknowledged, and it became a separate kingdom.

With all rights now equalised, the inhabitants of the remaining provinces of Spain differ as widely from one another as they do from the sister kingdom, while the folklore of Asturias and of the Basque Provinces is very closely allied with that of Portugal. To judge the Biscayan by the same standard as the Andaluz, is as sensible as it would be to compare the Irish squatter with Cornish fisher-folk, or the peasants of Wilts and Surrey with the Celtic races of the West Highlands of Scotland, or even with the people of Lancashire or Yorkshire.

Nor is it possible to speak of Spain as a whole, and of what she is likely to make of the present impulse towards national growth and industrial prosperity, without remembering that her population counts, among its rapidly increasing numbers, the far-seeing and business-like, if somewhat selfish, Catalan, with a language of his own; the dreamy, pleasure-loving Andaluz; the vigorous Basque, whose distinctive language is not to be learned or understood by the people of any other part of Spain; the half-Moorish Valencian and the self-respecting Aragonese, who have always made their mark in the history of their country, and were looked upon as a foreign element in the days when their kingdom and that of Leon were united, under one crown, with Castile.

It was only after Alfonso XII. had stamped out the last Carlist war that the ancient *fueros*, or special rights, of the Basque Provinces became a thing of the past, and their people liable to conscription, on a par with all the other parts of Spain.

Every student of history knows that the era of Spain's greatness was that of *Los Reyes Católicos*, Isabella of Castile and Ferdinand of Aragon, when the wonderful discovery and opening up of a new world made her people dizzy with excitement, and seemed to promise steadily increasing power and influence. Everyone knows that these dreams were never realised; that, so far from remaining the greatest nation of the Western World, Spain has gradually sunk back into a condition that leaves her to-day outside of international politics; and that, with the loss of her last colonies overseas, she appears to the superficial observer to be a dead or dying nation, no longer of any account among the peoples of Europe.

But this is no fact; it is rather the baseless fancy of incompetent observers, to some extent acquiesced in, or at least not contradicted, by the proud Castilian, who cares not at all about the opinions of other nationalities, and who never takes the trouble to enlighten ignorance of the kind. True, there was an exhibition of something like popular indignation when the people fancied they discovered a reference to Spain in the utterances of two leading English statesmen, during the war with America, and the feeling of soreness against England still to some extent exists; in fact, strange as it may appear, there is far less anger against America, which deprived Spain of her colonies, than against England, which looked on complacently, and with obvious sympathy for the aggressor. But all this is past, or passing. The Spaniards are a generous people, and no one forgets or forgives more easily or more entirely. Those who knew Madrid in the days of Isabel II. would not have imagined it possible that the Queen, who had been banished with so much general rejoicing, could, under any circumstances, have received in the capital a warm greeting; in fact, it was for long thought inexpedient to allow her to risk a popular demonstration of quite another character. But when she came to visit her son, after the restoration of Alfonso XII., her sins, which were many, were forgiven her. It was, perhaps, remembered that in her youth she had been more sinned against than sinning; that she was *muy Española*, kindhearted and gracious in manner, pitiful and courteous to all. Hence, so long as she did not remain, and did not in any way interfere in the government, the people were ready to receive her with acclamation, and were probably really glad to see her again without her *camarilla*, and with no power to injure the new order of things.

No nation in the world is more innately democratic than Spain—none, perhaps, so attached to monarchy ; but one lesson has been learned, probably alike by King and people—that absolutism is dead and buried beyond recall. The ruler of Spain, to-day and in the future, must represent the wishes of the people; and if at any time the two should once more come into sharp collision, it is not the united people of this once-divided country that would give way. For the rest, so long as the monarch reigns constitutionally, and respects the rights and the desires of his people, there is absolutely nothing to fear from pretender or republican. At a recent political meeting in Madrid, for the first time, were seen democrats, republicans, and monarchists united; amidst a goodly quantity of somewhat " tall " talk, two notable remarks were received with acclamation by all parties: one was that Italy had found freedom, and had made herself into a united nationality, under a constitutional monarch; and the other, that between the Government of England and a republic there was no difference except in name—that in all Europe there was no country so democratic or so absolutely free as England under her King, nor one in which the people so entirely governed themselves.

Among the many mistaken ideas which obtain currency in England with regard to Spain, perhaps none is more common or more baseless than the fiction about Don Carlos and his chances of success. A certain small class of journalists from time to time write ridiculous articles in English

papers and magazines about what they are pleased
to call the " legitimatist " cause, and announce its
coming triumph in the Peninsula. No Spaniard
takes the trouble to notice these remarkable pro-
ductions of the fertile journalistic brain of a foreigner. There are still, of course, people calling
themselves Carlists—notably the Duke of Madrid
and Don Jaime, but the cult, such as there is of
it in Spain, is of the " Platonic" order only,—to
use the Spanish description of it, " a little talk
but no fight,"—and it may be classed with the
vagaries of the amiable people in England who
amuse themselves by wearing a white rose, and
also call themselves " legitimatists," praying for
the restoration of the Stuarts.

The truth about the Carlist pretension is so
little known in England that it may be well to
state it. Spain has never been a land of the
Salic Law; the story of her reigning queens—
chief of all, Isabel la Católica, shows this. It
was not until the time of Philip V., the first of
the Bourbons, that this absolute monarch limited
the succession to heirs male by " pragmatic sanction"; that is to say, by his own unsupported
order. The Act in itself was irregular; it was
never put before the Cortes, and the Council of
Castile protested against it at the time.

This Act, such as it was, was revoked by
Charles IV.; but the revocation was never pub-
lished, the birth of sons making it immaterial.
When, however, his son Ferdinand VII. was

near his end, leaving only two daughters, he published his father's revocation of the Act of Philip V., and appointed his wife, Cristina, Regent during the minority of Isabel II., then only three years of age.

At no time, then, in its history, has the Salic Law been in use in Spain: the irregular act of a despotic King was repudiated both by his grandson and his great-grandson. Nothing, therefore, can be more ridiculous than the pretension of legitimacy on the part of a pretender whose party simply attempts to make an illegal innovation, in defiance of the legitimate kings and of the Council of Castile, a fundamental law of the monarchy. Carlism, the party of the Church against the nation, came into existence when, during the first years of Cristina's Regency, Mendizábal, the patriotic merchant of Cadiz and London, then First Minister of the Crown, carried out the dismemberment of the religious orders, and the diversion of their enormous wealth to the use of the nation. Don Carlos, the brother of Ferdinand VII., thereupon declared himself the Defender of the Faith and the champion of the extreme clerical party. *Hinc illæ lachrymæ*, and two Carlist wars!

The position of the Church, or rather what was called the "Apostolic party," is intelligible enough, and it is easy also to understand why Carlism has been preached as a crusade to English Roman Catholics, who have been induced in both Carlist wars to provide the main part of the funds

which made them possible; but to call Don Carlos
" the legitimate King " is an absurd misnomer.

For the rest, as regards Spain herself and the
wishes of her people, it is perhaps enough to remark that if, after the expulsion of the Bourbons
in 1868, at the time of the Revolution known as
" La Gloriosa," when Prim had refused to think
of a republic and declared himself once and
always in favour of a monarchy, and the Crown
of proud Spain went a-begging among the Courts
of Europe,—if, at that time of her national need,
Don Carlos was unable to come forward in his
celebrated character of " legitimate Sovereign of
the Spanish people," or to raise even two or three
voices in his favour, what chance is he likely to
have with a settled constitutional Government
and the really legitimate Monarch on the throne?
The strongest chance he ever had of success was
when the Basque Provinces were at one time disposed, it is said almost to a man, to take his side;
but, in fact, the men of the mountain were fighting much more for the retention of their own
fueros — for their immunity from conscription,
among others—than for any love of Don Carlos
himself. They would have liked a king and a
little kingdom all of their own, and, above all, to
have held their beloved rights against all the rest
of Spain.

All that, however, is over now. In all Spain
no province has profited as have those of the
North by the settled advance of the country.

Bilbao, once a small trading town, twice devastated during the terrible civil wars, has forged ahead in a manner perhaps only equalled by Liverpool in the days of its first growth, and is now more important and more populous than Barcelona itself; with its charming outlet of Portugalete, it is the most flourishing of Spanish ports, and is able to compare with any in Europe for its commerce and its rapid growth. Viscaya and Asturias want no more civil war, and the Apostolic party may look in vain for any more Carlist risings. More to be feared now are labour troubles, or the contamination of foreign anarchist doctrines; but in this case, the Church and the nation would be on the same side—that of order and progress.

In attempting to understand the extremely complex character of the Spaniard as we know him,—that is to say, the Castilian, or rather the Madrileño,—one has to take into account not only the divers races which go to make up the nationality as it is to-day, but something of the past history of this strangely interesting people. To go back to the days when Spain was a Roman province in a high state of civilisation: some of the greatest Romans known to fame were Spaniards—Quintilian, Martial, Lucan, and the two Senecas. Trajan was the first Spaniard named Emperor, and the only one whose ashes were allowed to rest within the city walls; but the Spanish freedman of Augustus, Gaius Julius Hyginus, had been made the chief keeper of the Palatine Library, and Ballus, another Spaniard, had reached the consulship, and had been accorded the honour of a public triumph. Hadrian, again, was a Spaniard, and Marcus Aurelius a son of Córdoba. No wonder that Spain is proud to remember that, of the " eighty perfect golden years " which Gibbon declares to have been the happiest epoch in mankind's history, no less than sixty were passed beneath the sceptre of her Cæsars.

The conquered had become conquerors; the intermarriage of Roman soldiers and settlers with Spanish women modified the original race; the Iberians invaded the politics and the literature of their conquerors. St. Augustine mourned the *odiosa cantio* of Spanish children learning Latin, but the language of Rome itself was altered by its Iberian emperors and literati; the races, in fact, amalgamated, and the Spaniard of to-day, to those who know him well, bears a strange resemblance to the Roman citizens with whom the letters of the Younger Pliny so charmingly make us familiar. The dismemberment of the Roman Empire left Spain exposed to the inroads of the Northern barbarians, and led indirectly to the subsequent Moorish inrush; for the Jews, harassed by a severe penal code, hailed the Arabs as a kindred race; and with their slaves made common cause with the conquering hordes.

The Goths seem to have been little more than armed settlers in the country. Marriage between them and the Iberians was forbidden by their laws, and the traces of their occupation are singularly few: not a single inscription or book of Gothic origin remains, and it seems doubtful if any trace of the language can be found in Castilian or any of its dialects. It is strange, if this be true, that there should be so strong a belief in the influence of Gothic blood in the race.

In all these wars and rumours of war the men of the hardy North remained practically unconquered. The last to submit to the Roman, the first to throw off the yoke of the Moor, the Basques and Asturians appear to be the representatives of the old inhabitants of Spain, who never settled down under the sway of the invader or acquiesced in foreign rule. Cicero mentions a Spanish tongue which was unintelligible to the Romans; was this Basque, which is equally so now to the rest of Spain, and which, if you believe the modern Castilian, the devil himself has never been able to master?

The history of Spain is one to make the heart ache. Some evil influence, some malign destiny, seems ever to have brought disaster where her people looked for progress or happiness. Her golden age was just in the short epoch when Isabella of Castile and Ferdinand of Aragon reigned and ruled over the united kingdoms: both were patriotic, both clever, and absolutely at one in their policy. It is almost impossible to us who can look back on the long records, almost always sad and disastrous, not to doubt whether in giving a new world "to Castile and Aragon," Cristobal Colon did not impose a burden on the country of his adoption which she was unable to bear, and which became, in the hands of the successors of her *muy Españoles y muy Católicos* kings, a curse instead of a blessing. Certain it is that Spain was not sufficiently advanced in political economy to understand or cope with the enormous changes which this opening up of a new world brought about. The sudden increase of wealth without labour, of reward for mere adventure, slew in its infancy any impulse there might have been to carry on the splendid manufactures and enlightened agriculture of the Moors; trade became a disgrace, and the fallacious idea that bringing gold and silver into a country could make it rich and prosperous ate like a canker into the industrial heart of the people, and with absolute certainty threw them backward in the race of civilisation.

Charles V. was the first evil genius of Spain; thinking far more of his German and Italian possessions than of the country of his mother, poor mad Juana, he exhausted the resources of Spain in his endless wars outside the country, and inaugurated her actual decline at a moment when, to the unthinking, she was at the height of her glory. The influence of the powerful nobility of the country had been completely broken by Isabella and Ferdinand, and the device of adopting

the Burgundian fashion of keeping at the Court
an immense crowd of nobles in so-called "waiting" on the Monarch flattered the national van-
ity, while it ensured the absolute inefficacy of the
class when it might have been useful in stemming
the baneful absolutism of such lunatics as Felipe
II. and the following Austrian monarchs, each
becoming more and more effete and more and
more mad. The very doubtful "glory" of the
reign of the Catholic Kings in having driven out
the Moors after eight centuries of conflict and
effort, proved, in fact, no advantage to the country;
but twenty thousand Christian captives were freed,
and every reader of history must, for the moment,
sympathise with the people who effected this free-
ing of their country from a foreign yoke.

Looking at the marvellous tracery of the church
of San Juan de los Reyes at Toledo, picked out by
the actual chains broken off the miserable Christian captives, and hanging there unrusted in the
fine air and sunshine of the country for over four
hundred years, one's heart beats in sympathy
with the pride of the Spaniards in their Catholic
Kings. But Toledo, alas! is dead; the centre of
light and learning is mouldering in the very
slough of ignorance, and Christianity compares
badly enough with the rule of Arab and Jew.

Nevertheless, it must be said that, had matters
been left as Isabella and Ferdinand left them,
Spain might have benefited by the example of her
conquerors, as other countries have done, and as

she herself did during the Roman occupation.
Philip II. was too wise to expel the richest and
most industrious of his subjects so long as they
paid his taxes and, at least, professed to be Christians. It was not until the reign of Philip III.
and his disgraceful favourite Lerma, himself the
most bigoted of Valencian "Christians," that, by
the advice of Ribera, the Archbishop of Valencia,
these industrious, thrifty, and harmless people
were ruthlessly driven out. They had turned
Valencia into a prolific garden,—even to-day it is
called the *huerta*,—their silk manufactures were
known and valued throughout the world; their
industry and frugality were, in fact, their worst
crimes; they were able to draw wealth from the
sterile lands which "Christians" found wholly
unproductive. "Since it is impossible to kill
them all," said Ribera, the representative of
Christ, he again and again urged on the King
their expulsion.

The nobles and landowners protested in vain.
September 22, 1609, is one of the blackest—perhaps, in fact, the blackest—of all days in the disastrous annals of Spain. The Marqués de Caracena,
Viceroy of Valencia, issued the terrible edict of
expulsion. Six of the oldest and "most Christian" Moriscos in each community of a hundred
souls were to remain to teach their modes of cultivation and their industries, and only three days
were allowed for the carrying out of this most
wicked and suicidal law. In the following six

months one hundred and fifty thousand Moors were hounded out of the land which their ancestors had possessed and enriched for centuries. Murcia, Andalucia, Aragon, Cataluña, Castile, La Mancha, and Estremadura were next taken in hand. In these latter provinces the cruel blunder was all the worse, since the Moors had intermarried with the Iberian inhabitants, and had really embraced the Christian religion, so called.

Half a million souls, according to Father Bleda, in his *Defensio Fidei*, were thrust out, with every aggravation of cruelty and robbery. No nation can commit crimes like this without suffering more than its victims. Spain has never to this day recovered from the blow to her own prosperity, to her commerce, her manufactures, and her civilisation dealt by the narrow-minded and ignorant King, led by a despicable favourite, and the fanatical bigot, Ribera. With the Moors went almost all their arts and industries; immense tracts of country became arid wastes: Castile and La Mancha barely raise crops every second year where the Moriscos reaped their teeming harvest, and Estremadura from a smiling garden became a waste where wandering flocks of sheep and pigs now find a bare subsistence. Nor was this all. Science and learning were also driven out with the Arab and Jew; Córdoba, like Toledo, vanished, as the centre of intellectual life. In place of enlightened agriculture, irrigation of the dry land, and the planting of trees, the peasant was taught

to take for his example San Isidro, the patron
saint of the labourer, who spent his days in prayer,
and left his fields to plough and sow themselves;
the forests were cut down for fuel, until the shade-
less wastes became less and less productive, and
the whole land on the elevated plains, which the
Moors had irrigated and planted, became little
better than a desert.

It was not only in the mother country that
frightful acts of bigotry and lust for wealth were
enacted. In Peru the Spaniards found a splendid
civilisation among the strange races of the Incas,
a condition of order which many modern states
might envy, a religion absolutely free from fetish
worship, and a standard of morality which has
never been surpassed. But they ruthlessly destroyed it all, desecrated the temples where the
sun was worshipped only as a visible representative of a God " of whom nothing could be known
save by His works," as their tenet ran, and sub-
stituted the religion which they represented as
having been taught by Jesus of Nazareth; a religion which looked for its chief power to the horrible Inquisition and its orgies called *Autos da fé!*

As regards the mysterious race of the Incas,
who in comparison with the native Indians were
almost white, and who possessed a high cultivation, it is curious to note that during the late
troubles in China records came to light in the
Palace of Pekin showing that Chinese missionaries
landed on the coast subsequently known as Peru,

in ages long antecedent to the discovery of the country by the Spaniards, and established temples and schools there. No one who reads the minute accounts of the Incas from Garcilaso de la Vega —himself of the royal race on his mother's side, his father having been one of the Spanish adventurers—can avoid the conclusion that the religion of the Incas, thus utterly destroyed by the Spaniards, was much more nearly that of Christ than the debased worship introduced in its place. The whole story of these "Children of the Sun," told by one of themselves afterwards in Córdoba, where he is always careful to keep on the right side of the Inquisition by pretending to be a "Christian after the manner of his father," is fascinatingly interesting as well as instructive.

It is almost impossible to speak of the Spanish Inquisition and its baneful influence on the people without seeming to be carried away by prejudice or even bigotry, but it is equally impossible for the ordinary student of history to read, even in the pages of the "orthodox," the terrible repression of its iron hand on all that was advancing in the nation; its writers, its singers, its men of science, wherever they dared to raise their voices in ever so faint a cry, ground down to one dead level of unthinking acquiescence, or driven forth from their native land, without ceasing to wonder at all at Spain's decadence from the moment she had handed herself over, bound hand and foot, to the Church. Wondering, rather, at her enormous inherent vitality, which at last, after so many centuries of spasmodic effort, has shaken off the incubus and regained liberty, or for the first time established it in the realms of religion, science, and general instruction.

It matters little or nothing whether the Inquisition, with its secret spies, its closed doors, its mockery of justice, and its terrible background of smouldering *Quemadero*, was the instrument of the Church or of the King for the moment. Whether a religious or a political tyranny, it was at all times opposed to the very essence of freedom, and it was deliberately used, and would be again to-day if it were possible to restore it, to keep the people in a gross state of ignorance and superstition. That it was admirable as an organisation only shows it in a more baneful light, since it was used to crush out all progress. Its effect is well expressed in the old proverb: " Between the King and the Inquisition we must not open our lips."

" I would rather think I had ascended from an ape," said Huxley, in his celebrated answer to the Bishop of Oxford, " than that I had descended from a man who used great gifts to darken reason." It has been the object of the Inquisition to darken reason wherever it had the power, and it left the mass of the Spanish people, great and generous as they are by nature, for long a mere mob of inert animals, ready to amuse themselves when their country was at its hour of greatest agony, debased by the sight of wholesale and cruel murders carried out by the priests of their religion in the name of Christ.

Even to-day the Spaniard of the lower classes can scarcely understand that he can have any part or parcel in the government of his country. Long ages of misrule have made him hate all governments alike: he imagines that all the evils he finds in the world of his own experience are the work of whoever happens to be the ruler for the time being; that it is possible for him to have any say in the matter never enters his head, and he votes, if he votes at all, as he is ordered to vote. He has been taught for ages past to believe whatever he has been told. His reason has been " offered as a sacrifice to God," if indeed he is aware that he possesses any.

The danger of the thorough awakening may be that which broke out so wildly during Castelar's short and disastrous attempt at a republic: that when once he breaks away from the binding power of his old religion, he may have nothing better than atheism and anarchism to fall back upon. The days of the absolute reign of ignorance and superstition are over; but the people are deeply religious. Will the Church of Spain adapt itself to the new state of things, or will it see its people drift away from its pale altogether, as other nations have done? This is the true clerical question which looms darkly before the Spain of to-day.

To return, however. The Austrian kings of

Spain had brought her only ruin. With the
Bourbons it was hoped a better era had opened,
but it was only exchanging one form of misrule
for another. The kings existed for their own
benefit and pleasure; the people existed to minister to them and find funds for their extravagance.
Each succeeding monarch was ruled by some up-
start favourite, until the climax was reached when
Godoy, the disgraceful Minister of Charles IV.,
and the open lover of his Queen, sold the country
to Napoleon. Then indeed awoke the great heart
of the nation, and Spain has the everlasting glory
of having risen as one man against the French
despot, and, by the help of England, stopped his
mad career. Even then, under the base and contemptible Ferdinand VII., she underwent the
" Terror of 1824," the disastrous and unworthy
regency of Cristina, and the still worse rule of her
daughter, Isabel II., before she awoke politically
as a nation, and, her innumerable parties forming
as one, drove out the Queen, with her *camarilla* of
priests and bleeding nuns, and at last achieved
her freedom.

For, whatever may be said of the last hundred
years of Spain's history, it has been an advance,
a continuous struggle for life and liberty. There
had been fluctuating periods of progress. Charles
III., a truly wise and patriotic monarch, the first
since Ferdinand and Isabella, made extraordinary
changes during his too short life. The population
of the country rose a million and a half in the

twenty-seven years of his reign, and the public
revenue in like proportions under his enlightened
Minister, Florida Blanca. No phase of the public
welfare was neglected: savings banks, hospitals,
asylums, free schools, rose up on all sides; va-
grancy and mendicancy were sternly repressed;
while men of science and skilled craftsmen were
brought from foreign countries, and it seemed as
if Spain had fairly started on her upward course.
But he died before his time in 1788, and was followed by a son and grandson, who, with their
wives, ruled by base favourites, dragged the
honour of Spain in the dust. Still, the impulse
had been given; there had been a break in the
long story of misrule and misery; Mendizábal and
Espartero scarcely did more than lighten the black
canopy of cloud overhanging the country for a
time; but at last came freedom, halting somewhat, as must needs be, but no longer to be repressed or driven back by the baneful influence
known as *palaciö*, intrigues arising in the immediate circle of the Court.

CHAPTER II

TYPES AND TRAITS

IT is the fashion to-day to minimise the influence of the Goths on the national characteristics of the Spaniard. We are told by some modern writers that their very existence is little more than a myth, and that the name of their last King, Roderick, is all that is really known about them. The castle of Wamba, or at least the hill on which it stood, is still pointed out to the visitor in Toledo, perched high above the red torrent of the rushing Tagus; but little seems to be certainly known of this hardy Northern race which, for some three hundred years, occupied the country after the Romans had withdrawn their protecting legions. On the approach of the all-conquering Moor, many of the inhabitants of Spain took refuge in the inaccessible mountains of the north, and were the ancestors of that invincible people known in Spain as "los Montañeses," from whom almost all that is best in literature, as well as in business capacity, has sprung in later years.

How much of the Celt-Iberian, or original inhabitant of the Peninsula, and how much of Gothic or of Teuton blood runs in the veins of the people of the mountains, it is more than difficult now to determine. It had been impossible, despite laws and penalties, to prevent the intermingling of the races: all that we certainly know is that the inhabitants of Galicia, Asturias, Viscaya, Navarro, and Aragon have always exhibited the characteristics of a hardy, fighting, pushing race, as distinguished from the Andaluces, the Valencianos, the Murcianos, and people of Granada, in whom the languid blood of a Southern people and the more marked trace of Arabic heritage are apparent.

The Catalans would appear, again, to be descendants of the old Provençals, at one time settled on both sides of the Pyrenees, though forming, at that time, part of Spain. Their language is almost pure Provençal, and they differ, as history shows in a hundred ways, from the inhabitants of the rest of Spain. The Castilians, occupying the centre of the country, are what we know as " Spaniards," and may be taken to hold a middle place among these widely differing nationalities, modified by their contact with all. Their language is that of cultivated Spain. No one dreams of asking if you speak Spanish; it is always: *Habla v Castellano?* And it is certainly a remnant of the old Roman, which, as we know, its emperors spoke " with a difference," albeit there are many traces of Arabic about it.

Even at the present day, when Spain is rapidly becoming homogeneous, the people of the different provinces are almost as well known by their trades as by their special characteristics. A *Gallego*—really a native of Galicia—means, in the common parlance, a porter, a water-carrier, almost a beast of burden, and the Galicians are as well known for this purpose in Portugal as in Spain, great numbers finding ready employment in the former country, where manual labour is looked upon as impossible for a native. The men of the lowest class emigrate to more favoured provinces, since their own is too poor to support them; they work hard, and return with their savings to their native hills. Their fellow-countrymen consider them boorish in manners, uneducated, and of a low class; but they are good-natured and docile, hard-working, temperate, and honest. "In your life," wrote the Duke of Wellington, "you never saw anything so bad as the Galicians; and yet they are the finest body of men and the best movers I have ever seen." There is a greater similarity between Galicia and Portugal than between the former and any other province of Spain.

Although they lie so close together, Asturias differs widely from its sister province both in the character of its people and its scenery. The Romans took two hundred years to subdue it, and the Moors never obtained a footing there. The Asturians are a hardy, independent race, proud of giving the title to the heir-apparent of the Spanish throne. The people of this province, like their neighbours the Basques, are handsome and robust in appearance; they are always to be recognised in Madrid by their fresh appearance and excellent physique. For the most part they are to be found engaged in the fish trade, while their women, gorgeously dressed in their native costume by their employers, are the nurses of the upper classes.

The ladies of Madrid do not think it " good style " to bring up their own children, and the Asturian wet nurse is as much a part of the ordinary household as the coachman or *mayordomo*. They are singularly handsome, well-grown women, and become great favourites in the houses of their employers; but, like their menkind, they go back to spend their savings among their beloved hills. Many of these young women come to Madrid on the chance of finding situations, leaving their own babies behind to be fed by hand, or Heaven knows how; they bring with them a young puppy to act as substitute until the nurse-child is found, and may be seen in the registry offices waiting to be hired, with their little canine foster-children. It is said that the Asturian women never part from the puppies that they have fed from their own breasts.

The Basque Provinces are, perhaps, the best known to English travellers, since they generally enter Spain by that route, and those staying in the south of France are fond of running across to have at least a look at Spain, and to be able to say they have been there. The people pride themselves on being "the oldest race in Europe," and are, no doubt, the direct descendants of the original and unconquered inhabitants of the Iberian Peninsula. In Guipuzcoa, the Basque may still be seen living in his flat-roofed stone house, of which he is sure to be proprietor, using a mattock in place of plough, and leading his oxen—for *bueyes* are never driven—attached to one of the heavy, solid-wheeled carts by an elaborately carved yoke, covered with a sheepskin. He clings tenaciously to his unintelligible language, and is quite certain that he is superior to the whole human race.

The *fueros*, or special rights, already spoken of, for which the Basques have fought so passionately for five hundred years, might possibly have been theirs for some time longer if they had not unwisely thrown in their lot with the Carlist Pretender. They practically formed a republic within the monarchy; but in 1876, when the young Alfonso XII. finally conquered the provinces, all differences between them and the other parts of the kingdom were abolished, and they had to submit to the abhorred conscription. With all the burning indignation which still makes some of them say, "I am not a Spaniard; I am a Basque," the extraordinary advance made in this part of Spain seems to show that the hereditary energy and talent of the people are on the side of national progress.

The distinctive dress of the Basques is now

almost a thing of the past; the bright kerchiefs of the women and the dark-blue cap (*bóina*) of the men alone remain. The Viscayan *bóina* has been lately introduced into the French army as the headgear of the Chasseurs and some other regiments.

"Aragon is not ours; we ought to conquer it!" Isabel la Católica is said to have remarked to her husband; and, indeed, the history of this little province is wonderfully interesting and amusing. It alone seems to have had the good sense always to secure its rights before it would vote supplies for the Austrian kings; whereas the other provinces usually gave their money without any security, except the word of the King, which was usually broken. Among the provisions of the *fueros* of the Aragonese was one that ran thus: "*Que siempre que el rey quebrantose sus fueros, pudiessen eligir otro rey encora que sea pagano*" (If ever the King should infringe our *fueros*, we can elect another King, even though he might be a pagan), and the preamble of the election ran thus: "We, who are as good as you, and are more powerful than you (*podemos mas que vos*) elect you King in order that you may protect our rights and liberties, and also we elect one between us and you (*el justicia*), who has more power than you: *y si no, no!*" which may be taken to mean, "otherwise you are not our King."

Somewhat of this spirit still abides in the Aragonese. The costume is one of the most pictur-

esque in Spain. The men wear short black velvet
breeches, open at the knees and slashed at the
sides, adorned with rows of buttons, and showing
white drawers underneath; *alpargatas*, or the
plaited hempen sandals, which, with the stockings, are black; a black velvet jacket, with
slashed and button-trimmed sleeves, and the
gaily-coloured *faja*, or silk sash, worn over an
elaborate shirt.

In the old days, when one entered Spain by
diligence from Bayonne to Pampeluna over the
Pyrenees, one learned something of the beauty of
the scenery and the healthy, hardy characteristics
of the people, as one whirled along through the
chestnut groves, over the leaping streams, always
at full gallop, up hill and down dale, with a precipice on one side of the road and the overhanging
mountains on the other. Below lay a fertile
country with comfortable little homesteads and
villages clustering round their church, and the like
dotted the hillsides and the valleys wherever there
seemed a foothold. As the diligence, with its
team of ten or twelve mules, dashed through
these villages or past the isolated farms, the people stood at their doors and shouted; it was evidently the event of the day. The mules were
changed every hour, or rather more, according
to the road, and as the ascent became steeper
more were added to their number; sometimes six
or eight starting from Bayonne where twelve or
fourteen were needed for the top of the Pass. At

least half the journey was always made at night, and if there were a moon the scenery became magically beautiful; but, in any case, the stars, in that clear atmosphere, made it almost as bright as day, while a ruddy light streamed from the lamp over the driver's seat, far above the coupé, along the string of hurrying mules, as they dashed round precipitous corners, dangerous enough in broad daylight. If one of the animals chanced to fall, it was dragged by its companions to the bottom of the gorge, where it would get up, shake itself, and prepare to tear up the next ascent as if nothing had happened.

A good idea could be formed of these hardy mountaineers in passing through their village homes. They are tall and good-looking, and seem to be simply overflowing with animal spirits. If it chanced to be on a Sunday afternoon, the priest, with his *sotana* tucked up round his waist, would be found playing the national game of *pelota* with his flock, using the blank wall of the church as a court.

One is apt to forget that Old Castile is one of the provinces having a northern sea-board. The inhabitants of this borderland are, to judge by appearance, superior to the people of the plains, who certainly strike the casual observer as being dirty and somewhat dull. The Castilian and Aragonese, however, may be said to constitute the heart of the nation. Leon and Estremadura form a part of the same raised plateau, but their people are very different. In speaking of the national characteristics, one must be taken to mean, not by any means the Madrileño, but the countrymen, whose homes are not to be judged by the *posadas*, or inns, which exist mainly for the muleteer and his animals, and are neither clean nor savoury.

"All the forces of Europe would not be sufficient to subdue the Castiles—*with the people against it*," was Peterborough's remark, and our Iron Duke never despaired "while the country was with him." He bore with the generals and the *Juntas* of the upper classes, in spite of his indignation against them, and, "cheered by the *people's support*," as Napier says, carried out his campaign of victory.

The ancient qualities of which the Castilians are proud are *gravedad, lealtad, y amor de Dios* —"dignity, loyalty, and love of God." No wonder that when the nation arises, it carries a matter through.

Estremadura, after the expulsion of the Moors, in whose days it was a fruitful garden, seems to have been forgotten by the rest of Spain; it became the pasturage for the wandering flocks of merino sheep, the direct descendants of the Bedouin herds, and of the pigs, which almost overrun it. Yet the remains of the Romans in Estremadura are the most interesting in Spain, and bear witness to the flourishing condition of the province in their day; moreover, Pizarro and

Cortes owe their birth to this forgotten land. The inhabitants of the southern provinces of Spain differ wholly from those of Castile and the north—they have much more of the Eastern type; in fact, the Valenciano or the Murciano of the *huerta*, the well-watered soil which the Moors left in such a high state of cultivation, in manners and appearance are often little different from the Arab as we know him to-day.

From the gay Andaluz we derive most of our ideas of the Spanish peasant; but he is a complete contrast to the dignified Castilian or the brusque Montañese. From this province, given over to song, dancing, and outdoor life, come — almost without exception—the bull-fighters, whose graceful carriage, full of power, and whose picturesque costume, make them remarkable wherever seen. Lively audacity is their special characteristic. *Sal* (salt) is their ideal; we have no word which carries the same meaning. Smart repartee, grace, charm, all are expressed in the word *Salada;* and *Salero* (literally, salt-cellar) is an expression met with in every second song one hears.

> Olé Saléro! Sin vanidad,
> Soy muy bonita, Soy muy Sala!

is the refrain of one of their most characteristic songs, *La moza é rumbo*, and may be taken as a sample:—

> Listen, Salero! without vanity,
> I am lovely—I am Salada!

3

During the *Feria* at Seville, the upper classes camp out in tents or huts, and the girls pass their time in singing and dancing, like the peasantry.

The Valencians are very different, being slow, quiet, almost stupid to the eye of the stranger, extremely industrious, and wrapped up in their agricultural pursuits. They fully understand and appreciate the system of irrigation left by the Moors, which has made their province the most densely populated and the most prosperous in appearance of all Spain.

A curious survival exists in Valencia in the *Tribunal de las Aguas*, which is presided over by three of the oldest men in the city; it is a direct inheritance from the Moors, and from its verdict there is no appeal.

Every Thursday the old men take their seats on a bench outside one of the doors of the cathedral, and to them come all those who have disputes about irrigation, marshalled by two beadles in strange, Old-World uniforms. When both sides have been heard, the old men put their heads together under a cloak or *manta*, and agree upon their judgment. The covering is then withdrawn, and the decision is announced. On one occasion they decreed that a certain man whom they considered in fault was to pay a fine. The unwary litigant, thinking that his case had not been properly heard, began to try to address the judges in mitigation of the sentence.

"But, Señores—" he began.

" Pay another peseta for speaking!" solemnly said the spokesman of the elders.

"*Pero, Señores*——"

"*Una peseta mas!*" solemnly returned the judge; and at last, finding that each time he opened his lips cost him one more peseta, he soon gave up and retired.

The Valencian costume for men consists of wide white cotton drawers to the knees, looking almost like petticoats, sandals of hemp, with gaiters left open between the knee and the ankle, a red sash, or *faja*, a short velvet jacket, and a handkerchief twisted turban-fashion round the head. The *hidalgos* wear the long cloak and wide sombrero common to all the country districts of Spain.

In speaking of Spaniards and their characteristics, as I have already said, we have to take into account the presence of all these widely differing races under one crown, and to remember that to-day there is no hard-and-fast line among the cultivated classes: intermarriage has fused the conflicting elements, very much for the good of the country, and rapid intercommunication by rail and telegraph has brought all parts of the kingdom together, as they have never been before. Education is now placed within reach of all, and even long-forgotten Estremadura is brought to share in the impulse towards national life and commercial progress. Comte Paul Vasili, in his charming *Lettres inédites* to a young diplomatist, first published in the pages of *La Nouvelle*

Revue, gives such an exact picture of the Spanish people, of whom he had so wide an experience and such intimate knowledge, that I am tempted to quote it in full.

" The famous phrase, *Á la disposicion de V.*, has no meaning in the upper ranks, is a fiction with the *bourgeoisie*, but is simple truth in the mouth of the people. The pure-blooded Spaniard is the most hospitable, the most ready giver in the world. He offers with his whole heart, and is hurt when one does not accept what he offers. He does not pretend to know anything beyond his own country . . . he exaggerates the dignity of humanity in his own person. . . . Even in asking alms of you he says: *Hermanito, una limosna, por el amor de Dios.* He does not beg; no, he asks, demands; and, miserable and in rags as he may be, he treats you as a brother— he does you the honour of accepting you as his equal. The Spaniard who has a *novia*, a guitar, a *cigarillo*, and the knowledge that he has enough to pay for a seat at the bull-fight, possesses all that he can possibly need. He will eat a plateful of *gazpacho* or *puchero*, a sardine, half a roll of bread, and drink clear water as often as wine. Food is always of secondary importance: he ranks it after his *novia*, after his *cigarillo*, after the bulls. Sleep? He can sleep anywhere, even on the ground. Dress? He has always his *capa*, and *la capa todo lo tapa*. The Spaniard is, above all things, *rumboso ;* that is to say, he has a large,

generous, and sound heart. . . . The masses
in Spain are perfectly contented, believing themselves sincerely to be the most heroic of people.
The Spaniard is naturally happy, because his
wants are almost *nil*, and he has the fixed idea
that kings—his own or those of other nations—
are all, at least, his cousins.''

This is not the place to speak at large of the religion of the people; but one remark one cannot
fail to make, and that is, the place which the
Virgin holds in the life and affections of the
masses. The name of the Deity is rarely heard,
except as an exclamation, and the Christ is spoken
of rather as a familiar friend than as the Second
Person in the Trinity; but the deep-seated love
for the Virgin, and absolute belief in her power
to help in all the joys and sorrows of life is one
of the strongest characteristics of this naturally
religious people. The names given at baptism
are almost all hers. Dolores, Amparo, Pilar,
Trinidad, Carmen, Concepcion,—abbreviated into
Concha,—are, in full, Maria de Dolores, del Pilar,
and so forth, and are found among men almost
as much as among women. The idea of the ever-
constant sympathy of the divine Mother appeals
perhaps even more strongly to the man, carrying
with it his worship of perfect womanhood, and
awakening the natural chivalry of his nature. Be
this as it may, the influence of the Virgin, and the
sincerity of her worship in every stage of life, in all
its dangers and in all its woes, is a religion in itself.

CHAPTER III

NATIONAL CHARACTERISTICS

CERTAIN strong characteristics of the Spanish people, with which the history of the world makes us well acquainted, are as marked in this hurrying age of railway and telegraph as ever they were in the past. One of the stupid remarks one constantly hears made by the unthinking tourist is: "Spain is a country where nothing ever changes." This is as true of some of the national traits of character as it is false in the sense in which the speaker means it. He has probably picked it out of some handbook.

Chief among these traits is dignity. The most casual visitor is impressed by it, sometimes very much to his annoyance, whether he finds it among the unlettered muleteers of Castile, the labourers of Valencia, or the present proprietor of some little Old-World *pueblo* off the ordinary route. The *mayoral* of the diligence in the old times, the domestic servant of to-day, the señora who happens to sell you fish, or the señor who mends your boots, all strike the same note—an absolute incapacity for imagining that there can be any

38

inequality between themselves and any other class, however far removed from them by the possession of wealth or education. Wealth, in fact, counts for nothing in the way of social rank; a poor *hidalgo* is exactly as much respected as a rich one, and he treats his tenants, his servants, all with whom he comes in contact, as brothers of the same rank in the sight of God as himself.

Bajo el Rey ninguno is their proverb, and its signification, that "beneath the King all are equal," is one that is shown daily in a hundred ways. The formula with which you are expected to tell the beggars—with whom, unfortunately, Spain is once more overrun—that you have nothing for them, is a lesson in what someone has well called the "aristocratic democracy" of Spain: "Pardon me, for the love of God, my brother," or the simple *Perdone me usted*, using precisely the same address as you would to a duke. It is no uncommon thing to hear two little ragged urchins, whose heads would not reach to one's elbow, disputing vigorously in the street with a *Pero no, Señor, Pero si, Señor*, as they bandy their arguments.

English travellers are sometimes found grumbling because the señor who keeps a wayside *posada*, or even a more pretentious inn in one of the towns, does not stand, hat in hand, bowing obsequiously to the wayfarer who deigns to use the accommodation provided.

This is one of the things in which Spain, to her

honour, *is* unchanged. The courtesy of her people, high or low, is ingrained, and if foreign—perhaps especially English and American—travellers do not always find it so, the fault may oftenest be laid to their own ignorance of what is expected of them, and to what is looked upon as the absolute boorishness of their own manners.

When a Spaniard goes into a shop where a woman is behind the counter, or even to a stall in the open market, he raises his hat in speaking to her as he would to the Duquesa de Tal y Fulano, and uses precisely the same form of address. The shopman lays himself at the feet of his lady customers—metaphorically only, fortunately, *Á los pies de V., Señora !*—with a bow worthy of royalty. She hopes that " God may remain with his worship" as she bids him the ordinary *Adios* on going away, and he, with equal politeness, expresses a hope that she may " go in God's keeping," while he once more lays himself at the señora's feet. All these amenities do not prevent a little bargaining, the one asking more than he means to take, apparently for the purpose of appearing to give way perforce to the overmastering charms of his customer, who does not disdain to use either her fan or her eyes in the encounter. The old woman will bargain just as much, but always with the same politeness. When foreigners walk in and abruptly ask for what they want with an air of immense superiority, as is the custom in our country, they are not unnaturally looked upon as *muy bruto*, and at the best it is accounted for by their being rude heretics from abroad, and knowing no better.

In Madrid and some of the large towns it is possible that the people have become accustomed to our apparent discourtesy, just as in some places —Granada especially—spoiled by long intimacy with tourists, the beggars have become importunate, and to some extent impudent; but in places a little removed from such a condition of modern "civilisation," the effect produced by many a well-meaning but ordinary Saxon priding himself on his superiority, and without any intention of being ill-bred or ill-mannered, is that of disgust and contemptuous annoyance.

No Spaniard will put up with an overbearing or bullying manner, even though he may not understand the language in which it is expressed; it raises in him all the dormant pride and prejudice which sleep beneath his own innate courtesy, and he probably treats the offending traveller with the profound contempt he feels for him, if with nothing worse. A little smiling and good-natured chaff when things go wrong, as they so often do in travelling, or when the leisurely expenditure of time, which is as natural to the Spaniard as it is irritating to our notions of how things ought to move, will go infinitely farther to set things right than black looks and a scolding tongue, even in an unknown language.

When English people come back from Spain

complaining of discourtesy, or what they choose to call insult, I know very well on whose head to fit the accusing cap, and it is always those people whose super-excellent opinion of themselves, and of their infinite importance at home, makes them certain of meeting with some such experience among a people to whom the mere expression " a snob" is by no means to be understood.

That railway travelling in Spain calls for a great exercise of patience from those accustomed to Flying Dutchmen and such-like expresses is quite true; though, by the way, many of the lines are in French hands, and served by French officials. It may safely be said, however, even at the present day, that those who are always in a hurry would do well to choose some other country for their holiday jaunt. A well-known English engineer, of French extraction, trying to get some business through in Madrid, once described himself as feeling " like a cat in hell, without claws." Perhaps the ignorance of the language, which constituted his clawless condition, was a fortunate circumstance for him. But that was a good while ago, and Madrid moves more quickly now.

Another characteristic of the Spaniard which awakens the respect and admiration of those who know enough of his past and present history to be aware of it is his courage: not in the least resembling the excitement and rush of mere conflict, nor the theatrical display of what goes by the name of " glory " among some of his neighbours; but the cool courage, the invincible determination which holds honour as the ideal to be followed all the same whether or not any person beyond the actor will know of it, and an unquestioning obedience to discipline, which call forth the ungrudging admiration of Englishmen, proud as we are of such national stories as that of our own *Little Revenge*, *The Wreck of the "Birkenhead*," or of " plucky little Mafeking," amongst hundreds of others.   Spaniards are rich in such inspiring memories, reaching from the earliest days of authentic history to the terrible episodes of the late war with America.   The story of Cervera's fleet at Santiago de Cuba is one to make the heart of any nation throb with pride in the midst of inevitable tears.

Again and again in reading Spanish history do we come upon evidences of this nobility of courage and disinterested patriotism.   It was the Spaniard Pescara who brushed the French army of observation from the line of the Adda, and marched his own forces and the German troops to the relief of Pavia.   All were unpaid, unclothed, unfed; yet when an appeal was made to the Spaniards, Hume tells us that they abandoned their own pay and offered their very shirts and cloaks to satisfy the Germans, and " the French were beaten before the great battle was fought."   They did precisely the same in the days of Mendizábal.

Again, in the height of Barbarossa's power, when Charles V., hoisting the crucifix at his masthead, led his crusading Spaniards against Goletta, and it fell, after a month's desperate siege, without pause or rest the troops, half dead with heat and thirst, pressed on to Tunis to liberate twenty thousand Christian captives. It was a splendid achievement, for the campaign was fought in the fierce heat of an African summer. Every barrel of biscuit, every butt of water, had to be brought by sea from Sicily, and as there were no draught animals, the soldiers themselves dragged their guns and all their provisions. It is, as we well know, no light task to find six weeks' supply for thirty thousand men with all our modern advantages; but these Spaniards did it when already exhausted, half fed, burnt up by the fierce African sun, and in face of an enemy well supplied with artillery and ammunition.

In the miserable time of Philip II., a garrison of two hundred men held out for months against a Turkish army of twenty thousand men at Mers-el-Keber; and the same heroic story is repeated at Malta, when the enemy, after firing sixteen thousand cannon shots in one month against the Christian forts, abandoned the siege in despair. Meanwhile the unspeakable bigot, Philip, was wasting his time in processions, rogations, and fasts, for the relief of the town, while he stirred no finger to help it in any effective manner.

These are stories by no means few and far between; the whole history of the race is full of such. We read of one town and garrison of eight thousand souls, abandoned by their king, starved, and without clothes or ammunition. Reduced at last to two thousand naked men, they stood in the breach to be slain to a man by the conquering Turk. Conqueror only in name, after all; for he who conquers is he who lives in history for a great action, and whose undaunted courage fires other souls long after he is at rest.

"But all this is very ancient history, of the days of Spain's greatness; now she is a decadent nation," says the superficial observer. The column of the *Dos de Mayo* on the Prado of Madrid, with its yearly memorial mass, shows whether that spirit is dead, or in danger of dying. The second of May is well called the "Day of Independence"; it was, in fact, the inauguration of the War of Independence, in which Spain gained enough honour to satisfy the proudest of her sons. The French had entered Madrid under pretence of being Spain's allies against Portugal, and Murat, once settled there to his own perfect satisfaction, made no secret of his master's intention to annex the whole peninsula. The imbecile King, Charles IV., had abdicated; his son, Ferdinand VII., was practically a captive in France. The country had, in fact, been sold to Napoleon, neither more nor less, by the infamous Godoy, favourite of the late King.

A riot broke out among the people on discovering that the French were about to carry off the

Spanish *Infantes.* The blood of some comparatively innocent Frenchmen was shed, and the
base governor and magistrates of Madrid allowed
Murat to make his own terms, which were nothing
less, in fact, than the dispersion of the troops, who
were ordered to clear out of their barracks, and
hand them over to the French. The two artillery
officers, Daoiz and Valarde, with one infantry
officer named Ruiz, and a few of the populace, refused, and, all unaided, attempted to hold the
barracks of Monteleon against the French army
of invasion! The end was certain; but little
recked these Spaniards of the old type. Daoiz
and Valarde were killed, the former murdered by
French bayonets after being wounded, on the
cannon by which they had stood alone against
the whole power of the French troops; Ruiz also
was shot. On the following day, Murat led out
some scores of the patriots who had dared to oppose him, and shot them on the spot of the Prado
now sacred to their memory. Thus was the torch
of the Peninsular War lighted. As one man the
nation rose; the labourer armed himself with his
agricultural implements, the workman with his
tools; without leaders, nay, in defiance of those
who should have led them, the people sprang to
action, and, with England's help, the usurper was
driven from the throne of France, and finally
caged in St. Helena. But it is never forgotten
that Spain—these two or three sons of hers pre-
ferring honour to life—has the glory of having

been the first to oppose and check the man and the nation that aspired to tyrannise over Europe.

It is not too much to say that the conduct of every individual in Cervera's fleet at Santiago de Cuba showed that the Spaniard's magnificent courage, his absolute devotion to duty, and his disregard of death are no whit less to-day than when those two thousand naked men stood in the breach to be slain in the name of their country's honour. The *Oquendo*, already a wreck, coming quietly out of her safe moorings in obedience to the insane orders of the Government in Madrid, steering her way with absolute coolness so as to clear the sunken *Diamante*, to face certain and hideous death, is a picture which can never fade from memory. It was said at the time by their enemies that there was not a man in the Spanish fleet that did not deserve the Victoria Cross; and this was all the more true because there was not even a forlorn hope: it was obedience to orders in the absolute certainty of death, and, what was harder still, with full knowledge of the utter uselessness of the sacrifice.

It is difficult to imagine that anyone can read the record of this heroic passage in the history of the Spain of to-day without a throb of admiration and pity. No wonder that the generous enemy went out of their way to do honour to the melancholy remnant of heroes as they mounted the sides of the American ironclads, prisoners of war.

Cervantes gave to the world a new adjective

when he wrote his romance of *The Ingenious Gentleman of La Mancha*—a world in which the filibusters are those of commerce, the pirates those of trade. When we English call an action "quixotic," we do not exactly mean disapproval, but neither, certainly, do we intend admiration; unless it be that of other-worldliness which it is well to affect, however far we may be from practising it ourselves. It is, at best, something quite unnecessary, if acknowledged to be admirable in the abstract. The quixotic are rarely successful, and success is the measure by which everything is judged to-day. Be that as it may, the more intimately one knows Spain, the more one becomes aware that what is with us an amiable quality of somewhat dubious value, is one of those which go to make up the Spaniard in every rank of life. His chivalry, his fine sense of honour, are nothing if not quixotic, as we understand the word; and just as in Scotland alone does one appreciate the characters in Sir Walter Scott's novels, so in Spain does one feel that, with due allowance for a spirit of kindly caricature, Don Quijote de la Mancha is not only possible, but it is a type of character as living to-day as it was when the genius of Cervantes distilled and preserved for all time that most quaint, lovable, inconsequent, and chivalrous combination of qualities which constitute a Spanish gentleman. Among her writers, her thinkers, her workers—nay, even now and then among her politicians—we come upon traits which remind us vividly of the ingenious gentleman and perfect knight of romance.

But this estimate of the Spanish character differs a good deal from the pictures drawn of it by the casual tourist; and it is scarcely surprising that it should be so. It has been well said that "the contrast between the ideal of honour and the practice of pecuniary corruption has always been a peculiar feature of Spain and her settlements." If we hear one thing oftener than another said of Spain, it is fault-finding with her public men; the evils of bribery, corruption, and self-seeking amongst what should be her statesmen, and, above all, her Government employees, are pointed out, and by none more than by Spaniards themselves. There is a good deal of truth at the bottom of these charges; they are the melancholy legacy of the years of misrule and of the darkness through which the country has struggled on her difficult way. No one looks for the highest type of character in any country among its party politicians. The creed that good becomes evil if it is carried out under one *régime*, and evil good under another, is not calculated to raise the moral perception; and it is only when a politician has convictions and principles which are superior to any office-holding, and will break with his party a hundred times sooner than stultify his own conscience, that he earns the respect of onlookers. There are, and have been, many such men among the politicians of Spain whose

4

names remain as watchwords with her people; but they have too often stood alone, and were not strong enough to leaven the mass and raise the whole standard of political integrity. Some of the highest and best men, moreover, have thrown down their tools and withdrawn from contact with a life which seemed to them tainted. But because Spain has done much in overthrowing her evil rulers and is struggling upwards towards the light, we expect wonders, and will not give time for what must always be a slow and difficult progress.

In Spain, everyone is a politician. The school-boy, who with us would be thinking of nothing more serious than football, aspires to sum up the situation and give his opinion of the public men as if he were an ex-prime minister at least. These orators of the *cafés* and the street corners are delighted to find a foreigner on whom they can air their unfledged opinions, and the traveller who can speak or understand a few words of Spanish comes back with wonderful accounts of what "a Spaniard whom I met in the train told me." In any case, no one ever says as hard things of his countrymen as a Spaniard will say of those who do not belong to the particular little political clique which has the extreme honour of counting himself as one of its number. These cliques—for one cannot call them parties—are innumerable, called, for the most part, after one man, of whom no one has heard except his particular friends,

Un Señor muy conocido en su casa, sobre todo á la hora de comer, as their saying is: "A gentleman very well known in his own house, especially at dinner-time."

Ford is answerable for many of the fixed ideas about Spain which it seems quite impossible to remove. Much that may have been true in the long ago, when he wrote his incomparable Guide Book, has now passed away with the all-conquering years; but still all that he ever said is repeated in each new book with unfailing certainty. Much as he really loved Spain, it must be confessed that he now and then wrote of her with a venom and bitterness quite at variance with his usual manner of judging things. It is in great part due to him that so much misunderstanding exists as to the Spanish custom of "offering" what is not intended to be accepted. If that peculiarity ever existed—for my part, I have never met with it at any time—it does so no longer. When a Spaniard speaks of his house as that of "your Grace" (*su casa de Usted*), it is simply a figure of speech, which has no more special meaning than our own "I am delighted to see you," addressed to some one whose existence you had forgotten, and will forget again; but nothing can exceed the generous hospitality often shown to perfect strangers in country districts where the accommodation for travellers is bad, when any real difficulty arises.

It is customary, for instance, in travelling, when you open your luncheon-basket, to offer to share its contents with any strangers who may chance to be fellow-passengers. Naturally, it is merely a form of politeness, and, in an ordinary way, no one thinks of accepting it—everyone has his own provision, or is intending to lunch somewhere on the way; but it is by no means an empty form. If it should chance, by some accident, that you found yourself without—as has happened to me in a diligence journey which lasted twenty hours when it was intended only to occupy twelve —the Spanish fellow-travellers will certainly insist on your accepting their offer. Also, if they should be provided with fresh fruit—oranges, dates, or figs—and you are not, their offer to share is by no means made with the hope or expectation that you will say *Muchas gracias*, the equivalent of " No, thank you."

What is really difficult and embarrassing sometimes is to avoid having pressed on your acceptance some article which you may have admired, in your ignorance of the custom, which makes it the merest commonplace of the Spaniard to "place it at your disposition," or to say: " It is already the property of your Grace." Continued refusal sometimes gives offence. The custom of never doing to-day what you can quite easily put off till to-morrow is, unfortunately, still a common trait of Spanish character; but as the Spaniard is rapidly becoming an alert man of business, it is not likely that that will long remain one of the national characteristics. Time in old days seemed

of very little value in a country where trade was
looked upon as a disgrace, or at least as unfitting
any one to enter the charmed circle of the first
Grandeza; but that is of the past now in Spain,
as in most countries.   To be sure, it has not there
become fashionable for ladies to keep bonnet-shops
or dress-making establishments, nor to open afternoon tea-rooms or *orchaterias*, still less to set up
as so-called financiers, as it has with us.   However, even that may come to pass in the struggle
for "*el* high life," of which some of the Spanish
writers complain so bitterly.   Imagination absolutely refuses, however, to see the Spanish woman
of rank in such surroundings.

For the rest, the Spanish woman, wherever you
meet her, and in whatever rank of society, is devout, naturally kind-hearted and sympathetic,
polite, and entirely unaffected; a good mother,
sister, daughter; hard-working and frugal, if she
be of the lower class; fond above all things of
gossip, and of what passes for conversation; light-
hearted, full of fun and harmless mischief; born
a coquette, but only with that kind of coquetry
which is inseparable from unspoiled sex, with no
taint of sordidness about it; and, before all things,
absolutely free from affectation.   Their own expression, *muy simpatica*, gives better than any
other the charm of the Spanish woman, whether
young or old, gentle or simple.

It was the possession of all these qualities in a
high degree by Doña Isabel II. that covered the

multitude of her sins, and made all who came within her influence speak gently of her, and think more of excuses than of blame. It is these qualities which give so much popularity to her daughter, the Infanta Isabel, who, like her mother, is above all things *muy Española*. That the Spanish woman is passionate, goes without saying; one only has to watch the quick flash of her eye—"throwing out sparks," as their own expression may be translated—to be aware of that. While the eyes of the men are for the most part languid, only occasionally flashing forth, those of the women are rarely quiet for a moment; they sparkle, they languish, they flame — a whole gamut of expression in one moment of time; and it must be confessed that they look upon man as their natural prey.

CHAPTER IV

SPANISH SOCIETY

THERE is something specially charming about Spanish society, its freedom from formality, the genuine pleasure and hospitality with which each guest is received, and the extreme simplicity of the entertainment. In speaking, however, of society in Madrid and other modern towns, it must be remembered that the old manners and customs are to a great extent being modified and assimilated with those of the other Continental cities. A great number of the Spanish nobility spend the season in Paris or in London as regularly as any of the fashionable people in France or England. There is no country life in Spain, as we understand the word; those of the upper ten thousand who have castles or great houses in the provinces rarely visit them, and still more rarely entertain there. A hunting or a shooting party at one of these is quite an event; so when the great people leave Madrid, it is generally to enter into London or Paris society, and, naturally, when they are at home they to a great extent retain cosmopolitan customs. At the foreign legations or ministries also, society loses much of its specially Spanish character.

The word *tertulia* simply means a circle or group in society; but it has come to signify a species of "At Home" much more informal than anything we have in the way of evening entertainment. The *tertulia* of a particular lady means the group of friends who are in the habit of frequenting her drawing-room. The Salon del Prado is the general meeting-place of all who feel more inclined for *al fresco* entertainment than for close rooms, and the different groups of friends meeting there draw their chairs together in small circles, and thus hold their *tertulia*. The old Countess of Montijo was so much given to open-handed hospitality, and it was so easy for any English person to obtain an introduction to her *tertulia*, that her daughter, the Empress Eugénie, used to call it the *Prado cubierto*—"only the Prado with a roof on." It is not customary for anything but the very lightest of refreshments to be offered at the ordinary *tertulia*, and this is one of its great charms, for little or no expense is incurred, and those who are not rich can still welcome their friends as often as they like without any of the terrific preparations for the entertainment which make it a burden and a bore, and without a rueful glance at the weekly bill afterwards. Occasionally, chocolate is handed round, and any amount of tumblers of cold water. The chocolate is served in small coffee-cups, and is of the consistency of oatmeal porridge; but it is delicious all the same, very light and well frothed up. It is " eaten " by dipping little finger-rusks or sponge-chips into the mixture, and you are extremely glad of the glass of cold water after it. This is, however, rather an exception; lemonade, *azucarillas* and water, or tea served in a separate room about twelve o'clock, is more usual. The *azucarilla* is a confection not unlike " Edinburgh rock," but more porous and of the nature of a meringue. You stir the water with it, when it instantly dissolves, flavouring the water with vanilla, lemon, or orange, as well as sugar. Sometimes you are offered meringues, which you eat first, and then drink the water.

I have a very perfect recollection of my first *tertulia* in Madrid, when I was a very young girl. We had been asked to go quite early, as we were the strangers of the evening. Between seventy and eighty guests dropped in, the ladies chiefly in morning dress, as we understand the word. A Spanish lady never rises to receive a gentleman; but when any ladies entered the large drawing-room where we were all seated, every one rose and stood while the new arrivals made the circuit of the room, shaking hands with their friends or kissing them on both cheeks, and giving a somewhat undignified little nod to those whom they did not know. The first time every one rose I thought we were going to sing a hymn, or take part in some ceremony; but as it had to be repeated each time a lady entered the room, I began to wish they would all come at once. As soon as the dancing began, however, this ceremony was discontinued. When you are introduced to a partner, the first thing he does is to inquire your Christian name; from that time forth he addresses you by it, as if he had known you from infancy, and in speaking to him you are expected to use his surname alone. If there be more than one brother, you address the younger one as "Arturo," "Ramon," or whatever his Christian name may be. The diminutives are, however, almost always used—Pacquita, Juanito, etc., in place of Francisca or Juan. Even the middle-aged and old ladies are always spoken to by their Christian names, and it is quite common to hear a child of six addressing a lady who is probably a grandmother as "Luisa" or "Mariquita."

Between the dances the pauses were unusually long, but they were never spent by the ladies sitting in rows round the walls, while the men blocked up the doorways and looked bored. There were no "flirting corners," and sitting out on the stairs à deux would have been a compromiso. The whole company broke up into little knots and circles, the chairs, which had been pushed into corners or an ante-room, were fetched out, and the men, without any sort of shyness, generally seated themselves in front of the ladies, and kept up a perfectly wild hubbub of conversation until the music for the next dance struck up. Dowagers

and *dueñas* were few; they sat in the same spot
all the evening, and asked each other what rent
they paid, how many *chimeneas* (fireplaces) they
had, whether they burned wood or coal, and la-
mented over the price of both. They reminded
one irresistibly of the " two crumbly old women "
in *Kavanagh* " who talked about moths, and cheap
furniture, and the best cure for rheumatism."

The dances were the same as ours, with some
small differences: the *rigodon* is a variation of the
quadrille, and the lancers are slightly curtailed.
There was a decided fancy for the polka and a
species of mazurka, which I remembered having
learned from a dancing-master in the dawn of life,
under some strange and forgotten name. Spaniards dance divinely—nothing less. They waltz
as few other men do, a very poetry of motion, an
abandonment of enjoyment, as if their soul were
in it, especially if the music be somewhat languid.
This is especially the case with the artillery
officers, who are great favourites in society, and
belong exclusively to the upper ranks.

I have described this *tertulia* at length because
it was a typical one of many. The cotillon was
a great favourite, and generally closed the evening. I always had an idea that one cause of its
popularity was the extended opportunities it gave
for a couple who found each other's company
pleasant to enjoy it without much interference.
It rather made up for the loss of the staircase and
the window-seats, or balconies, dear to English

dancers. The rooms are generally kept in a
stifling state of heat, a thick curtain always hanging over the door, and never an open window or
any kind of ventilation; this, however, does not
inconvenience the Spaniard in the least. It is
usual to smoke during the intervals of the dances
—cigarettes as a rule; but I have often known a
man to lay his cigar on the edge of a table, and
give it a whiff between the rounds of a *valse* to
keep it going.

This, however, is the Spanish *tertulia*. You
are "offered the house" once and for always, and
told the evenings on which your hostess "re-
ceives," generally once, sometimes many more
times in the week; then you drop in, without
further invitation, whenever you feel inclined;
after the opera, or on the days when there is no
opera, or on your way from the theatre, or at any
hour. This sort of visiting puts an end to what
we, by courtesy, call "morning calls." There is
always conversation to any amount, generally
cards, music, and, when there are sufficient young
people, a dance.

There is no exclusiveness and no caste about
Spanish society; all the houses are open, and the
guests are always welcome. There are, of course,
the houses of the nobility, and there are many
grades in this *Grandeza*, some being of very recent creation, others of the uncontaminated *sangre
azul;* but there is no hard-and-fast line. The
successful politician or the popular writer has the

entrée anywhere, and there is no difficulty about going into the very best of the Court society, if one has friends in that *tertulia*. One guest asks permission to present his or her friend, the permission is courteously granted, and the thing is done. Poets and dramatists are in great request in Madrid society. It is the custom to ask them to recite their own compositions, and as almost every Spaniard is a poet, whatever else he may be, there is no lack of entertainment. All the popular authors—Campoamor, Nuñez de Arce, Pelayo, Valera, and many others—may thus be heard; but the paid performer (so common in London drawing-rooms) of music, light drama, or poetical recitation, is probably absolutely unknown in Madrid society.

During the season balls are given occasionally at the Palace, and at the houses of the great nobility, the Fernan-Nuñez, the Romana, the Medinaceli, and others, whose names are as well known in Paris and London as in Madrid. Dinner-parties are also becoming much more common in private houses than they were before the Restoration, and as for public dinners, they are so frequent that they bid fair to become of the same importance as the like institution in England. Costume balls, dances, dinners, and evening entertainments among the *corps diplomatique* abound. Everyone in Madrid has a box or stall at the Teatro Real, or opera-house, and many ladies make a practice of " receiving " in their *palcos;* and in the en-

trance-hall, after the performance is over, an hour
may be spent, while ostensibly waiting for carriages, in conversation, gossip, mild flirtation, and
generally making one's self agreeable among the
groups all engaged in the same amusement.
Almost everyone, also, whatever his means may
be, has an *abono* at one or other of the numerous
theatres, sometimes at more than one; and if it
be a box, the subscribers take friends with them,
or receive visits there. It is a common thing,
either in the opera-house or in the theatres, for a
couple of friends to join in the *abono ;* in this case
it is arranged on which nights the whole box or
the two or three stalls shall be the property of
each in turn. Besides paying for the seats, there
is always a separate charge each night made for
the *entrada*—in the Teatro Real it is a peseta and
a half, in the others one peseta. By this arrangement anyone can enter the theatre by paying the
entrada, and take chance of finding friends there,
frequently spending an hour or so going from one
box to another. All this gives the theatre more
the air of being an immense "At Home" than
what we are accustomed to in England. The intervals between the acts are very long, and, as all
the men smoke, somewhat trying.

Spanish women are great dressers, and the costumes seen at the race-meetings at the Hippodrome, and in the Parque, are elaborately French,
and sometimes startling. The upper middle class
go to Santander, Biarritz, or one of the other

fashionable watering-places, and it is said of the
ladies that they only stop as many days as they
can sport new costumes. If they go for a fortnight they must have fifteen absolutely new
dresses, as they would never think of putting one
on a second time. They take with them immense
trunks, such as we generally associate with American travellers; these are called *mundos* (worlds)
—a name which one feels certain was given by
the suffering man who is expected to look after
them.

There are many little details in Spanish life,
even of the upper classes, which strike one as
odd. One, for instance, is the perfect *sangfroid*
with which they pick their teeth in public; but
so little is this considered, as with us, a breach of
good manners, that the dinner-tables are supplied
with dainty little ornaments filled with tooth-
picks, and these are handed round to the guests
by the waiters towards the close of the meal. Nor
is it an unknown thing for a Spanish lady to spit.
I have seen it done out of a carriage window in
the fashionable drive without any hesitation. At
the same time, as one of the great charms of a
Spanish woman is the total absence in her of anything savouring of affectation, one would far
sooner overlook customs that are unknown in
polite society with us than have them lose their
own characteristics in an attempt to imitate the
social peculiarities of other nations that have
incorporated the ominous word " snob " in their

vocabularies. It has no equivalent in the language of Castile, and it is to be hoped will never be borrowed. Nevertheless, a recent Spanish writer laments the fact that in the race for "*el* high life" his fellow-countrywomen "are not ashamed to drink whisky!" We have yet to learn that whisky-drinking among women is an element of good style in any class of English society. The idea that Spanish ladies were in the habit of smoking in past times is a mistake. If they do so now it is an instance of the race for "*el* high life," of which the writer quoted above complains.

In imitation of foreign customs, many of the ladies in Madrid and the more modern cities have established their " day " for afternoon visitors. After all, this is but the Spanish *tertulia* at a different hour, but if it should ever supersede the real evening *tertulia* it will be a thousand pities; it would be far more sensible if we were to adopt the Spanish custom, rather than that they should follow ours. In the evening, the hour varying, of course, with the time of year, all Madrid goes to drive, ride, or walk in the Buen Retiro, now called the Parque de Madrid. It is beautifully laid out, with wide, well-kept roads and well-cared-for gardens; it has quite superseded the Paseo de la Fuente Castellano, which used to be the " Ladies' Mile " of Madrid.

Madrid is a city of which one hears the most contradictory accounts. The mere traveller not uncommonly pronounces it "disappointing, uninteresting, less foreign than most Continental capitals,"—"everything to be seen at best second-rate France," etc., etc. The Museo, of course, must be admired,—even the most ignorant know that to contemn that is to write themselves down as Philistines;—but for the rest, they confess themselves glad to escape, after two or three days spent in La Corte, to what they fancy will prove more interesting towns, or, at any rate, to something which they hope will be more characteristic. But those who settle in Madrid, or know it well, winter and summer, and have friends among its hospitable people, come to love it, one might almost say, strangely, because it is not the love that springs from habit or mere familiarity, but something much warmer and more personal. One charm it has, which is felt while there and pleasantly remembered in absence—its much-maligned climate. The position of Madrid at the apex of a high table-land, two thousand one hundred and sixty feet above the level of the sea, with its wide expanse of plain on every hand but that on which the Guadarramas break the horizon with their rugged, often snow-capped, peaks, naturally exposes it to rapid changes of temperature; that is to say, that if the snow is still lying on the Sierra, and the wind should chance to blow from that direction on Madrid, which is steeped in sunshine winter and summer for far the greater part of the year, there is nothing to break its course,

5

and naturally, a Madrileño, crossing from the sheltered corner, where he has been " taking the sun," to the shady side of the street and the full force of the chilly blast, will be very likely to " catch an air," as the Spaniard expresses it. But that *tan sutil aire de Madrid*, which Ford seems to have discovered, and which every guide-book and slip-shod itinerary has ever since quoted, might very well now be allowed to find a place in the limbo of exploded myths; it has done far more than its duty in terrifying visitors quite need-lessly. That *pulmonia fulminante* (acute pneu-monia) is a very common disease among the men of Madrid, there is no doubt, and in the days when Ford wrote, they were no doubt immediately bled, and so hastened on their way out of this troublesome world by the doctors; but one has not very far to seek for the cause of this scourge when one notices the habits of the Madrileño. In the first place he hates nothing quite so much as fresh air, and the cafés, clubs, taverns, and places where he resorts are kept in such a state of heated stuffiness that it seems scarcely an exaggeration to say that the air could be cut out in junks, like pieces of cake. If he travel by train, all windows must be kept closely shut, while he smokes all the time. When, at last, it is necessary to brave the outer air in order to reach home, he, carefully and before leaving the vitiated atmosphere he has been breathing, en-velops himself in his cloak, throwing the heavy cape, generally lined with velvet or plush, across his mouth and nose, barely leaving his eyes visible; he thus has three or four folds of cloth and velvet as a respirator. It often happens that at the corner of some street the long arm of the icy "Guadarrama" reaches him; a sudden gust of wind plucks off his respirator, and the mischief is done. But should he reach the safe closeness of his own house, he has certainly done his level best to charge his lungs with unwholesome and contaminated air.

You have only to see the women on the coldest day in winter with nothing over their heads but a silk or lace mantilla, or a mere *velo* of net, and the working-women with nothing but their magnificent hair, or, at most, a kerchief, to be certain that it is not the "air" that is to blame. I have seen the women going about Madrid in winter, both by day and night, when the men were muffled to the eyes, with thicker dresses, of course, and perhaps a fur cape, but no sort of wrap about their head or throat; and *pulmonia* is comparatively unknown among women. To English people, accustomed to plenty of fresh air and water, Madrid has never been an unhealthy place, and it is extremely probable that one of these days our doctors will be sending their consumptive patients there for the winter. They might easily do worse.

One of the coldest winters I remember in Madrid, a young Englishman came out with a letter of introduction from friends. He looked as if he had not many weeks to live, and in truth he was condemned by his doctors, and his hours were numbered. He was a Yorkshireman by birth, but had some years past developed seeds of consumption. He had been sent year after year to Madeira and other of the old resorts, having been told that a winter in England would certainly finish him. Finally, he made his doctors tell him the truth: it was that he had not many months, perhaps not many weeks, to live.

"Very well, then," he replied, "there is no use worrying any more about my health. I shall do my best to enjoy the little time I may have left." He threw all his medicines and remedies out of the window, he looked out for the most unhealthy place he could find, where he would be most certain of never meeting another consumptive patient; and in the course of the search he came across the well-worn chestnut about the air of Madrid. "That is the place for me," he exclaimed; "only strong and healthy people can live there. At any rate, so long as I do live, I shall be amongst sound lungs, and shall see no more fellow-sufferers. The *aire tan sutil* will kill me, and that will be the end of the matter." So far from killing him, the fine champagne-like air of Madrid went as near curing him as was possible for a man with only one lung. He took no precautions, never wrapped up, went out at night as well as by day, and when he died, fourteen years later, it was not of consumption. He used to come to Madrid for the winter to escape the damp of England, and revelled in the warmth and freshness of that sun-steeped air.

The climate of Madrid has sensibly altered since I have known it, and will continue to do so as vegetation increases and trees spring up and grow to perfection within and around it. In the old times, before the splendid service of water of the Lozoya Canal was in common use, the air was so dry as to make one's skin uncomfortable, and one's hair to break off into pieces like tinder under the brush; there was also a constant thickening in the throat, causing slight discomfort, and a penetrating, impalpable dust which nothing ever laid, and which formed a veritable cloud reaching far above the heads of the promenaders in the Salon del Prado. A very short time changed all this. Twice a day the streets were watered with far-reaching hose, a constant stream ran about the stems of the trees in the Prado, gardens were planted and constantly watered, and while the hitherto barren, dust-laden places began to blossom as the rose, the air itself became softer, less trying, and, perhaps, there is rather more uncertainty about the weather, or at any rate a greater rainfall. At one time there were but two rainy seasons—spring and autumn—and never a cloud in between. For about three days clouds would be gathering gradually in the sky, beginning with one literally " no bigger than a man's hand."

Whenever there was a cloud, you might be certain of rain, past or to come. Then one day, when there was no longer any blue to be seen, the heavens opened and the rain came down. There could be no mistake about it. When it rains or thunders in Madrid, it tries to get it all over as quickly as possible. There is nothing like doing a thing well when you are about it, and Madrid thoroughly understands this matter of rain. It never ceases, never tempts people to go out and then drowns them. No, if you go out, it is with a thorough understanding of what you are undertaking; and if you are disposed to be critical about anything in the municipal management of La Corte now, try to imagine what it was when the water from the roofs was carried out in wide pipes a few feet from the edge, and allowed to pour on the heads of the defenceless foot-passengers, or almost to break in the roof of carriage or cab which had to pass under them. This is the time to learn why the bridges over the Manzanares are so wide and so strong; not one whit too much of either, if they are to withstand the mighty onrush. We used to go off to the Casa de Campo the moment the rain was over, for the sake of seeing Madrid as one never sees it at other times— its magnificent Palace crowning the steep bluff, round which a mighty river is rushing to the sea.

The rain lasts a week, a fortnight, or even more, and then the sky takes at least three days to clear, during which it resembles our English white-flecked blue, or its hurrying grey masses, and the cloud-shadows fly over the wide landscape, now all suddenly changed to verdure, and lie on the distant *sierra*, giving an unwonted charm to the scene. The Casa de Campo, the Florida, and all green spots become carpeted with wild flowers; the trees seem to have put on new leafage, so fresh are they and free from the overloading of dust. And then, gradually, the Manzanares repents him of his anger and haste; no more foam is dashing against the piers of the bridges, no more crested waves are hurrying before the wind; he sinks gently and slowly back to his accustomed lounging pace, "taking the sun" with lazy ease once more; and the washerwomen come down and resume their labours under the plane trees; and there is no more thought of rain for many a week, perhaps month, to come; and that strangely deep, impenetrable vault of a blue unknown elsewhere spreads its canopy over a clean, rain-washed city.

The Parque de Madrid, which lies high above the Prado, affords a striking view of the country on all sides. An Englishman of wide Continental experience, describing this prospect, says he was "more than recompensed by the sudden apparition, through an opening between the houses, of the exquisite *campagna* that surrounds Madrid. . . . Compared with that of Rome, it seemed to me clearer, and more extensive, while the hue of the atmosphere that overspread it was of a rich

purple.'' I have quoted these remarks because
it is so rare for English visitors, accustomed to
the lush green of our own meadows and woods,
to find anything to admire in what is too often
called the '' mangy,'' or at best the '' arid,'' surroundings of the capital of Spain. This, however, was written in September, and there had
been heavy rains; after the crops are gathered
and before the autumn rains come on, the prospect
is scarcely so much to be admired. That the
view is extensive, no one can deny; there is un-
broken horizon, except where the rugged peaks
of the Guadarramas pierce the sky, and the at-
mospheric effects are often marvellously beautiful, especially when the swift shadows of clouds
pass over the wide landscape, or lie upon the
''everlasting hills.''

For myself, this vast expanse, with the sense of
immensity which we generally are only able to
associate with the sea, has always had an extraordinary charm. I have seen it at all times of the
year, early in the morning, and at, or just before,
sundown—nay, even once or twice by moonlight,
or with the marvellous blue vault overhead, that
seems so much higher and greater there than elsewhere, studded with planet and star, luminous
beyond all that we know in our little island,
where the blue is so pale by comparison, and the
atmosphere laden with moisture when we think
it most clear. I do not remember elsewhere in
Spain, or in any other country, such a depth of

sky or such brilliancy of moon and star light as in Madrid, where it is as easy to read by night as by day on some occasions.

Given plenty of water, and Madrid is an ideal place for flowers. Such carnations as those which are grown in the nursery gardens there are never seen elsewhere—they are a revelation in horticulture; nor are the roses any less wonderful. The bouquet with which a Spaniard, whether *hidalgo* or one of your servants, greets your birthday is generally a pyramid almost as tall as yourself. It needs to be placed in a large earthenware jar on the floor, and if you should be happy enough to have a good many friends, there is scarcely room for anything else in your *gabinete*. The flowers one can raise in a balcony in Madrid merely by using plenty of water, syringing the dust off the leaves, and shading them occasionally from the worst heat, are more than equal to anything a hothouse in England can produce. An idea may be formed of the really marvellous fertility of the soil and climate by the rapidity with which seeds develop. I remember one summer, when some of the new gardens were being laid out in the Buen Retiro, a grand concert and evening *fête* was to be given as the opening function. On the evening before this entertainment was to take place we happened to be near, and strolled in to see how the preparations were going on. The gravel walks were all there, the stands for the bands, the Chinese lanterns hanging from the trees, but where was the grass? Alas! wherever it ought to have been were to be seen brown, sad-looking patches of bare earth, not a blade springing anywhere; what was worse, an army of gardeners were, at that moment only, sowing the seed in some patches, while others were being rolled, and watered with hose. *Cosa de España!* of course. It had been put off to *mañana*, until now there might be *fête*, but no gardens. The following evening, when in company with all Madrid we went to the concert, behold a transformation! Soft, green, velvety sward—not to be walked on, it is true, but lovely to behold—covered the patches so absolutely bald twenty-four hours ago. The seed we had seen sown had sprung up as thickly as finest cut velvet. *Cosa de España*, indeed! It is not always in Spain —the land of the unexpected—that *Mañana verémos* is foolishness.

Until after Christmas the winter in Madrid is charming, even if it be cold; the glorious sunshine from dawn to sunset, the fine exhilarating air, raise one's spirits unconsciously; but very often the old year is dead before any real cold comes on. I have sat out in the Buen Retiro many a day in December with book or work, and scarcely any more wrap than one wears in summer in England. After that there is generally a cold, and perhaps disagreeable, spell, when the wind comes howling across the plains straight from the snow and ice, and the Madrileño thinks it terrible; as a matter of fact, so long as the sky remains clear, there is always one side of the street where one can be warm. Sometimes, but not often, the cold weather or the bitter winds last pretty far into the spring, and it has certainly happened in the depth of the frost that one of the sentries on duty at the Palace, on the side facing the mountains, was found frozen to death when the relief came. After that the watch was made shorter, and the change of guard more frequent in winter. I have seen the Estanque Grande in the Retiro covered with ice several inches thick; but as all Madrid turned out to see the wonder and watch the foreigners skate, a thing that appeared never to have been seen before, it could not have been a very common occurrence.

Riding early in the morning in winter outside Madrid, even with the sun shining brightly and a cloudless sky, the cold was often intense, especially in the dells and hollows. We have often had to put our hands under the saddle to keep them from freezing, so as to be able to feel the reins, and if I were riding with the sun on the off-side, my feet would become perfectly dead to feeling. But what an air it was! Something to be remembered, and long before we reached home we were in a delicious glow. The horses, English thoroughbreds, enjoyed it immensely, and went like the wind. I have been in Madrid in every part of the year, and never found it unbearably hot, though one does not generally wait for July or

August; but here again the lightness and dryness of the air seem to make heat much easier to bear. Numbers of Madrid people think nothing of remaining there all the summer through.

CHAPTER V

MODERN MADRID

MADRID has grown out of all knowledge in the last thirty years. No one who had not seen it since the time of Isabel II. would recognise it now, and even then much had been done since Ferdinand VII. had come back from his fawning and despicable captivity in France—where he had gloried in calling himself a " French prince "—to act the despot in his own country. The Liberal Ministers who, for short periods, had some semblance of power during the regency of Cristina had done a little to restore the civilisation and light established by Charles III., and wholly quenched in the time of his unworthy and contemptible successors. But even in 1865, the Alcalá Gate, standing where the Plaza de la Independencia is now, formed one boundary of Madrid, the Gate of Atocha was still standing at the end of the *paseo* of that name, and the Gate of Sta. Barbara formed another of the limits of the city. The Museo was unfinished and only to be entered by a side door, encumbered with builders' rubbish and half-hewn blocks of stone.

The Paseo of la Fuente Castellana ended the Prado, and not a house was to be seen beyond the Mint, or outside the Gate of Alcalá.

All the town outside these barriers has arisen since; the magnificent viaduct across the Calle de Segovia, the Markets, the Parque de Madrid, the Hippodrome, the present Plaza de Toros, all are new. The old Bull Ring stood just outside the Alcalá Gate, and all beyond it was open country; no *casas palacias* along the Fuente Castellana, no Barrio Salamanca. Madrid has, however, always been a cheerful, noisy, stirring city, full of life and the expression of animal spirits. In days not so very long past the streets were filled with picturesque costumes of the provinces, with gaily decorated mules and donkeys carrying immense loads of hay or straw, or huge nets filled with melons or pumpkins, almost hiding everything but the head and the feet of the animal; or a smart-looking "Jacket" man from the country districts would go whistling by, Asturians, Murcians, Gallegos, gypsies, *toreros* in their brilliant *traje* Andaluz—always to be recognised by their tiny pigtails of hair, and by their splendidly lithe and graceful carriage—all these jostling, singing, chaffing each other, while the jingling bells on innumerable horses, mules, donkeys, rang through the sunlit air, and made the Puerta de Sol and the streets branching from it a constant scene of life and gaiety. Now and then would come the deep clang of the huge bell of the draught oxen, drawing their Old-World carts, often with solid discs of wood for wheels, while the women of the lower class sported their brilliantly embroidered Manila shawls, chattered, and fluttered their gaily-coloured fans just like the other señoritas. Mantillas, even then, were only to be seen on old ladies; but the smart little *velo* coquettishly fastened with a natural flower adorned all the young girls — French millinery, which never suits a Spanish face, being kept for the evening *paseo*. It is a pity these national costumes have gone out of fashion. A Spanish girl with *velo* and fan is something quite superior to the same fascinating young person dressed after the style of Paris— with a difference; for there is always a difference.

Madrid, in fact, is becoming cosmopolitan, and is little to be distinguished from other capitals, except in the *barrios bajos* on the national *fiestas*, and wherever the country people, as distinguished from the Madrid work-people, congregate. These last are rapidly losing all picturesqueness, dressing just as the workers in any other capital dress. They are, perhaps, still no less *gatos* (cats), those of them at least who have had the honour of being born in La Corte, this being the name given them by their fellow country-people.

If it be meant as a term of reproach, the Madrileño has an excellent answer in giving the history of its origin. In the reign of Alfonso VI., during one of the many war-like operations of this King, he wished to take an important and difficult fortress, and had collected all his forces to attack it — the Madrileños alone were late; it was, in fact, only the day before the assault was to take place that they arrived upon the scene. The King was furious, and when their leader approached his Majesty to know where the troops were to bivouac for the night, he replied that there was no room in his camp for laggards; pointing to the enemy's fortress, he added: "*There* will be found plenty of lodging for those who come too late for any other." Saluting his Majesty very courteously, the soldier withdrew, understanding thoroughly the indirect sneer at the valour of his troops; he went back to his regiment, summoned his officers and men, and repeated to them the King's word. One and all agreed that they would, in fact, seek their night's lodging just where the King had indicated. Impossible as the feat appeared, they instantly rushed to the attack of the formidable fortress with such irresistible dash that they succeeded in scaling the walls and entering it, pikes in rest. The King, who had run forward as soon as he heard of the attack, watched with delight his loyal Madrileños climbing up the face of the masonry with extraordinary skill, and not a little loss.

"Look, look!" he cried to those near him. "See how they climb! They are cats!"

The other forces at once came to their assistance, the fortress fell into the King's hands before nightfall, and those who had been in " no hurry " to join the army found their lodgings within it, as his Majesty had contemptuously recommended them to do. His anger was forgotten in admiration and praise; and, from that time, all those born in Madrid have the right to call themselves *gatos*.

It is curious how the observation of those who know Spain intimately differs—one must suppose according to temperament. Thus Antonio Gallenga, the well-known correspondent of the *Times*, who really knew Spain well, has left it on record that the people are not musical, and that he never remembers to have heard any of them singing in the streets, or at their work. I do not know how this could have happened, unless our old friend did not recognise the singing he did hear as music, for which he might, perhaps, be forgiven. My own experience is that the people are always singing, more or less, if you agree to call it so. As the houses are almost all built in flats, many of the windows open into *patios*, or court-yards, large or small, as the case may be. You may reckon on always having two or three servants, male or female, at work in the *patio*, the women washing or scrubbing, the men probably cleaning their horses, carriages, or harness; but whatever else they may be doing, you may be quite certain they will all be singing, though it is equally certain that, by the greatest exercise of amiability, you could scarcely call the result a song; the

6

words seem to be improvised as the performer
goes on. There was a light-hearted groom in
one of the *patios* of our flat, in the Calle Lope de
Vega, who would continue almost without a
break the whole day. An old friend who used to
amuse himself by listening to this remarkable
performer declared that if he started his song in
the early morning with a stick that was thick
enough, he would go on till midnight telling the
world in general all the people he had killed with
it, and the other wonders of Hercules it had performed.

The ditty always begins on a high note, and
goes quavering irregularly downwards, with
infinite twirls, shakes, and prolonged notes,
these being sung to the exclamation "Ay!"
Minor keys enter a good deal into this kind
of performance, and the most remarkable part
of it is that the singer, once having reached
the bottom of the scale—for there is no end—
is able to begin again on the same high note,
and hit upon, more or less, the same variations
a second time. If you have nothing better to
do than to listen to some of these improvis-
atores, you will get a long, and more or less
connected, history of some event; but it takes a
long time—and, perhaps, is not often worth the
expenditure. The songs which you hear to the
accompaniment of the guitar are different from
these, though the introduction of the " Ay!" and
the frequent shakes and twirls are always there.

The working Madrileño's ideal of happiness is to go a little way along one of the dusty *caminos reales* (highways) to some little *venta*, or tavern, or to take refreshments out in baskets. They will sit quite contentedly in the dust by the side of the road, or in a field of stubble or burnt-up grass, to eat and drink, and then the guitar comes into play, and the dancing begins. It is always the *jota aragonesa*, which is not so much dancing as twirling about slowly, and, it would almost seem, sadly; but there is always a circle of admiring lookers-on, who beat time with stamping of feet and clapping of hands, and watch the performance as eagerly as if there were something quite fresh and new about it. Occasionally, these parties go out by omnibus or tram, as far as they can, and then start their picnic repast, to be followed by the inevitable dance and song, just wherever they happen to be.

One of the most curious sights of Madrid is the great wash-tub of the Manzanares. As you descend the steep bluff on which the city stands, towards the river, you find the banks covered with laundresses, kneeling at short distances from one another, each scrubbing the clothes on one board, which slopes down into the water, while another board, fixed so as to stand out into the stream, or a little embankment made of sand, dams up the scanty supply of water she can obtain. As the Manzanares in summer is divided into a great number of small streams, this scene is repeated on the edge of each one, while the expanse of sand which occupies the centre of what ought to be the river-bed is one forest of clothes-props, with all the wash of Madrid hanging on the lines. On the banks the children, in the intervals of school, are playing bull-fights, or some of their innumerable dancing and singing games; the women are one and all performing the gradual descent of the gamut with variations called singing; and above all is the glorious sun, transfiguring all things, and throwing deep, purple shadows from the high plane-trees along the banks.

The road which runs along the bank of the Manzanares, at the farther side from Madrid, is a revelation to those who only know the plains through which the railway from the north passes, and which for the greater part of the year, except when the crops are growing, are quite as arid as we are accustomed to suppose. On the left lies the Casa de Campo, an immense extent of park, containing, on the high ground, some splendid specimens of the Scotch fir, and, in more sheltered spots, groves of beech, avenues of plane, and masses of the dark-leaved ilex, which grows to great perfection in this climate. The "Florida," another of the royal properties, lies to the right, and a splendid road shaded by majestic trees, and with wide, grassy margins, stretches away to the village of El Pardillo, where Longfellow established his quarters, and which he describes in his

Outre Mer, and from that on to the forest, or whatever you may call it, of El Pardo, where there is a royal residence now but seldom used, you may ride for many hours and still find yourself in this wild park, which many of the inhabitants of Madrid have never seen. Here one can realise a little how the city may have once been a hunting lodge of the Kings, as we are told. The Pardo may be reached through the Casa de Campo, a gate at the extreme end of the principal drive leading into the forest.

Up on the high ground of the Casa de Campo there is a splendid view of Madrid, with the Palace crowning the steep bluff overhanging the Manzanares. It was in the " country house " itself, near the gate, that our " Baby Charles " is said to have climbed the high wall of the court-yard to get a glimpse of the Infanta whom he hoped to make his wife. When I knew the place intimately, on the very highest part of the Park was a large enclosure of the wild forest, railed in with high wooden palisading. Within this lived a flock of ostriches, belonging to the Crown. No one seemed to know anything about them, nor how long they had been there. What puzzled us much was how they were fed, or if they were left to cater for themselves. One thing I can answer for: they were very wild, and very ferocious; the moment they saw our horses coming up the hill they would run from all parts of the enclosure trying their best to get at us,

striking with their feet and wings, and uttering
gruesome shrieks.   It was one of our amusements
to race them, keeping outside their high fence
while they strode over the ground, their necks
stretched out, and their absurd wings flapping
after the manner of a farmyard gander; but, with
the best efforts, the horses were never able to
keep up the pace for long; the birds invariably
won, and we left them screeching and using language that did not appear to be parliamentary,
when they found that the fence was the only
thing that did not give in, as they craned their
necks and stamped in their baffled rage.   The
horses, at first rather afraid of the birds, soon
learned to enjoy the fun, and raced them for all
they were worth.   I do not know if this strange
colony is still settled there.

A curious feature of Spanish country life to us
are the goatherds.   Where the large flocks of
goats about Madrid pasture, I know not; but I
have often seen them coming home in the evening to be milked, or starting out in the morning.   The goatherd, clad in his *manta*, and
carrying a long wand of office over his shoulder,
and I think also a horn, stalks majestically along
with all the dignity of a royal marshal of processions, and the goats follow him, with a good deal
of lagging behind for play, or nibbling, if they
should chance to see anything green.   Still, they
scamper after their *generalissimo* in the end, and
meanwhile he is much too dignified to look back.

Taking advantage of this, I have seen women come out of their cottages on the roadside and milk a goat or two as it passed; and from the way the animal made a full stop, and lent itself to the fraud—if such it were—it was evidently a daily occurrence.

In times not long past, if indeed they do not still exist, the dust-heaps outside Madrid were the homes of packs of lean, hungry dogs, great brindled creatures of the breed to be seen in Velasquez pictures; these animals prowled about the streets of Madrid in the early morning, acting as scavengers. When they became too numerous, the civil guards laid poison about at night in the dust-heaps before the houses, and the very early riser might see four or five of these great creatures lying dead on the carts which collect the refuse of Madrid before the world in general is astir. These wild dogs were disagreeable customers to meet when riding outside the city, until we learned to avoid the localities where they spent their days, for they would give chase to the horses if they caught sight of them, and the only thing to be done was to remain perfectly quiet until they tired of barking and returned to the dust-hills to resume their search for food.

The description of peasant life in Madrid would be incomplete if we left unmentioned the daily siesta in the sun of the Gallegos and lower-class working-men. On the benches in the Prado, on the pavement, in the full blaze of the sun, these men will stretch themselves and sleep for an hour or two after their midday meal. I have seen the Gallego porters make themselves a hammock with the rope they always carry with them—*mozos de cuerda* they are called—literally slinging themselves to the *reja* or iron bars of the window of some private house, and sleep soundly in a position that would surely kill any other human being. "Taking the sun" (*tomando el sol*) is, however, the custom of every Spaniard of whatever degree.

The casual visitor to Madrid is always struck with the number of carriages to be seen in the *paseo;* but the fact is that everyone keeps a carriage, if it be at all possible, and it is no uncommon thing for two or three *pollos* to join together in the expense of this luxury, and a sight almost unknown to us is common enough in Madrid—young men, the "curled darlings" of society, lazily lounging in a Victoria or Berlina in what is known as the "Ladies' Mile." The Madrid *pollo* is not the most favourable specimen of a Spaniard ; the word literally means a "chicken," but applied to a young man it is scarcely a complimentary expression, and has its counterpart with us in the slang terms which from time to time indicate the idle exquisite who thinks as much of his dress and his style as any woman does or more. The Madrid *pollo* often is, or ought to be, a schoolboy, and the younger he is, naturally, the more conceited and impertinent

he is. It is curious that with the feminine termination, this word (*polla*) loses all sense of banter
or contempt; it simply means a young girl in the
first charm of her spring-time.

Riding in the Row has always been a favourite
pastime in Madrid, but to English ideas the *pollo*
is more objectionable there than elsewhere, since
his idea of riding is to show off the antics of a
horse specially taught and made to prance about
and curvet while he sits it, his legs sticking out
in the position of the Colossus of Rhodes, his
heels, armed with spurs, threatening catastrophe
to the other riders. An old English master of
foxhounds, who was a frequent visitor in Madrid,
used to compare the Paseo of the Fuente Castellana at the fashionable hour to a "*chevaux de frise
on horseback.*" These gentlemen must not, however, be supposed to represent Spanish horsemanship. Ladies ride a good deal in the Paseo, but
one cannot call them good horsewomen. To get
into the saddle from a chair, or a pair of stable
steps, and let their steed walk up and down for
an hour or so in the Row, is not exactly what we
call riding. If you hire a carriage in Madrid you
are so smart that your best friends would not
recognise you. A grand barouche and pair dashes
up to your door, probably with a ducal coronet
on the panels. The coachman and footman wear
cockades, and the moment you appear they both
take off their hats and hold them in their hands
until you are seated in the carriage. This cere-

mony is repeated every time you alight, the
coachman reverently uncovering as you leave the
carriage or return to it, as well as the footman
who is opening the door for you.

It is most comforting; royalty, I feel sure, is
nothing to it! We will not look critically at the
lining of the noble barouche, nor at the varnish on
its panels, still less make disagreeable remarks
about the liveries, which do not always fit their
wearers—it is economical to have liveries made a
good medium size, so that if the servants are
changed the clothes are not;—one can always feel
grateful for the polite and agreeable attendants.
How oddly it must strike the Spaniards in England to notice the stolid indifference of "Jeames
de la Plush," and the curt tap of his first finger
on the brim of his hat as his lady enters her carriage or gives her directions!

All the mules, and most of the horses, ponies,
or donkeys ridden by the "Jacket" men or
country people are trained to pace instead of to
trot; it is said to be less fatiguing on a long journey. The motion as you ride is, to our notions,
very unpleasant, being a kind of roll, which at
first, at any rate, gives one the feeling of sea-
sickness. The animal uses the fore and hind feet
together alternately, as he literally runs over the
ground. It does not appear to be a natural pace,
but is carefully taught, and, once acquired, it is
very difficult to break the animal of it; his idea of
trotting has become quite lost; nor is it a pretty

action, nor one suited to show off good qualities—
it has always something of a shuffle about it. If
it has its advantages, except that stirrups may be
dispensed with, they are not very apparent to
those accustomed to the usual paces of an English
horse. Personally, I disliked it particularly.

There have been many efforts to introduce
racing, with its contingent improvement in the
breed of horses, perhaps the earliest during the
regency of Espartero; but these ended, as most
things did in the old days when Spain was only
beginning her long struggle for freedom, in failure and loss to the enterprising gentlemen—of
whom the then Duque de Osuna was one—who
spent large sums of money in the effort. The
old race-course of that time lay somewhere in the
low ground outside Madrid on the course of
the Manzanares; many a good gallop I have had
on it, though it was abandoned and forgotten
long ago by the Madrileños. At the present
time horse-racing may be said to have become
naturalised in Spain under the *Sociedad del Fomento de la Cria Caballar* (Society for the Encouragement of Horse-breeding), and all that concerns
horsemanship is naturally improved and improving.

A good idea of Spanish horses may be gained
by a visit to the Royal Mews in Madrid. There
are the cream-coloured horses from the royal
stud at Aranjuez, *jacuitas* from Andalucia, as
well as the mountain ponies of Galicia. Those

who have never seen the Spanish mule have no
idea what the animal is—powerful, active, graceful, and almost impossible to injure. They are
used in the royal stables and in those of the
nobility, for night work, since they are so hardy
as not to be injured by long waiting in the cold
or wet. They are the correct thing in the carriages of the Papal Nuncio and all ecclesiastics,
and are generally preferred to horses for long or
difficult journeys. They are a great feature in
the army; kept in splendid condition and of great
size, they not only drag the heavy guns, but in
the celebrated mountain artillery each mule carries a small gun on his back. A brigade of this
arm would have been invaluable to the British in
South Africa, having no doubt had its initiation in
the guerilla warfare of Spain's frequent civil wars.

The clipping of mules and donkeys, which are
also very superior animals to anything we know
by that name, is in the hands of the gypsies, who
have a perfect genius for decorating their own
animals and any others committed to their man-
ipulation. Only the upper part is shaved, or
clipped to the skin, the long winter coat being
left on the legs and half-way up the body. Generally, on the shoulders and haunches a pattern is
made by leaving some of the hair a little longer;
the figure of the cross with rays is not uncommon,
but it is wonderful how elaborate and beautiful
some of these patterns are, looking as if embossed
in velvet on the skin. One day, passing a *venta*

in a street in Madrid, we were attracted by a gaily-decked donkey standing outside. He had the words, *Viva mi Amo* (Long live my Master!), finished with a beautiful and artistic scroll pattern, in rich velvet across his haunches. While we stood admiring this work of art, the master within laughingly warned us that the ass kicked if anyone came near him. Perhaps the elaborate decoration was a practical joke!

The mules and donkeys which come in from the country are generally very picturesque, with a network of crimson silk tassels over their heads, and a bright-coloured *manta* thrown across their sleek, glossy backs. These *mantas* serve many purposes; they are made of two breadths of brightly striped and ornamented material of wool and silk, sewn up at one end, or sometimes for some distance at each end, like a purse; sometimes they are thrown across the mule to serve as saddle-bags, sometimes one end is used as a hood and is drawn over the master's head, while the remainder is thrown across his chest and mouth and over the left shoulder. The best of these *mantas* are elaborately trimmed at both ends with a deep interlacing fringe, ending in a close row of balls, and have a thick ornamental cord sewn over the joining. These, which are intended for human wraps and not as saddle-bags, are only sewn up at one end, so as to form something very like the old monkish hood. All the horses, mules, donkeys, and oxen wear bells: the oxen have

generally only one large bronze bell, which
hangs under the head; the others have rows of
small jingling silver or brass bells round their
collars or bridles.

These draught oxen are beautiful animals,
mostly a deep cream in colour, with dark points,
magnificent eyes, and a sphinx-like look of
patience, as if biding their time for something
much better to come. Their harness is not apparently irksome to them, and is not so heavy as
one sees on the Portuguese oxen, for instance.
They are coupled by a wooden bar across the
head, and their driver, if such he can be called—
rather, perhaps, the guide—walks in front with a
long stick, possibly a wand of office, over his
shoulder to show them the way. The dress of
this functionary is picturesque: a wide-brimmed
hat (*sombrero*), a shirt, short trousers to the
knees, with gaiters of woven grass (*esparto*), a
faja round his waist, and *manta* thrown over his
shoulder if cold. He stalks majestically along,
followed by his equally majestic *bueyes*, and one
wonders of what all three are thinking as they
trudge along the sun-smitten roads, regardless of
dust or of anything else. The cars are rude
enough, and the wheels sometimes solid discs of
wood. Occasionally, a hood of bent pieces of
wood covered with linen is fixed. Tame oxen, or
cabestros, as they are called, play a very important
part in the *ganaderos* and the bull-rings. They
appear to be held in some sort of superstitious

reverence, or strange affection, by the poor beasts who only live to make sport for men. In driving the bulls from one pasture to another, or bringing them into the towns, the *cabestros* are followed with unwavering faith by these otherwise dangerous animals; where the *cabestro* goes, clanging his great bell, the bull follows, and while under the charge of his domesticated friend he is quite harmless.

At one time, the bulls used to be driven to the bull-ring outside Madrid in specially made roads sunk some fifteen feet below the level of the fields, and paved. Along these the *pastor*, or shepherd, and *picadores*, armed with long lances, went with the *cabestros* and the herd of bulls to be immolated. I have frequently met this procession when riding, either in the early morning or late evening, outside Madrid; but so long as the *cabestros* are present, there is nothing to fear, for the bulls are perfectly quiet and harmless. Once, however, riding with a friend, I had a disagreeable and exciting adventure. We were quietly walking our horses along the Ronda de Alcalá, when we heard an immense amount of shouting, and suddenly became aware that we ourselves were the objects of the excitement, waving of hands, screaming, and gesticulating. Before we had time to do more than realise that we were being warned of some terrific danger in wait for us round the corner of the high wall, some little distance in advance, two *picadores* on horseback, armed with their long pikes, galloped round the corner, also shouting wildly to us, and pointing across the fields as if telling us to fly, and almost at the same moment the whole drove of bulls, tearing along at a terrific rate, without *cabestros*, appeared, charging straight towards us. We did not need a second hint. At one side of the road was the old wall of Madrid, at the other a high bank with a wide ditch beyond it. Without a word, we put our horses at the bank,—they had realised the situation as quickly as we had,—jumped the ditch at a flying leap from the top of the bank, and were off across a field of young wheat. Once only I looked behind, and saw a magnificent black bull, with his tail in the air—a signal of attack—on the top of the bank over which I had just leaped, preparing to follow me. Long afterwards, as it seemed, when my horse slackened his pace, I found myself alone in a wide plain, neither bulls nor fellow-rider to be seen. His horse had bolted in another direction from mine, and we heard afterwards that the *picadores* had galloped in between me and the sporting bull and turned him back. Eventually, the *cabestros* appeared on the scene, and the poor misguided bulls were inveigled into the shambles for the *fiesta* of the morrow. How they had ever managed to break away or gain the public road at all, we were never able to learn.

CHAPTER VI

THE COURT

DURING the reign of Don Alfonso XII., except during the interval when the melancholy death of his first beloved Queen, Mercédes, plunged King, Court, and people into mourning, Madrid was gayer than perhaps it has ever been. No one loved amusement better than the young King, who was only seventeen when the military *pronunciamiento* of Martinez Campo called him to the throne from which his mother had been driven seven years previously. He had taken his people, and indeed all the world, by storm, for from the first moment he had shown all the qualities which make a ruler popular, and Spain has never had a young monarch of so much promise. He had the royal gift of memory, and an extraordinary facility in speaking foreign languages; it was said that the Russian and the Turkish envoys were the only ones with whom he was unable to converse as freely in their languages as in his own. He was an excellent speaker, always knew the right thing to say, the best thing to do to gain the hearts of his people, and to make himself agreeable

to all parties and all nationalities alike. He
was the first King of Spain to address his people
de usted in place of *de tu*, a mark of respect which
they were not slow to appreciate; he was a
modern, in that he would go out alone, either on
foot or riding, allowed applause in his presence
at the theatres, unknown before, and himself
would salute those he knew from his box. He
gave audience to all who asked, was an early
riser, devoted to business when it had to be performed, was an enthusiast in all military matters,
and, perhaps better than all in the eyes of his
people, he was devoted to the bull-ring. Extremely active, resolute, firm, fond of all kinds of
active sports, such as hunting and shooting,
equally fond of society, picnics, dances, and all
kinds of entertainments, he seemed destined to
become the idol of his people, and to lead his beloved country back to its place in Europe. His
death, when only twenty-seven, changed all this.
Queen Maria Cristina has been a model wife,
widow, mother, and Regent. She was devoted
to her husband, and though it was said at first to
be a political marriage, contracted to please the
people, it was undoubtedly a happy one. The
Queen has scarcely taken more part in public life
during her sad widowhood than Queen Victoria
did. She has devoted herself to her public duties
as Regent and to the education and care of her
children.

Alfonso XIII., born a king after his father's

death, has always been rather a delicate boy; his mother has determined that his health and his education shall be the first and chief care of her life, and nothing turns her from this purpose. If she has never been exactly popular, she has at least the unbounded respect and admiration of the people. She does not love the " bulls," and, therefore, she is not *Española* enough to awaken enthusiasm; she keeps the boy King too much out of sight, so that his people scarcely know him, even in Madrid; but this is the very utmost that anyone has to say against her, while all shades of politicians, even to declared Republicans, speak of her with respect and with real admiration of her qualities of heart and mind.

All Court gaieties are, however, at an end. Once a year or so a ball at the palace, a formal dinner, or reception, when it cannot be avoided— that is all, and for the rest the Queen is rarely seen except at religious ceremonies or state functions, and the King, never. He is supposed to take his amusements and exercise in the Casa de Campo, and rarely crosses Madrid.

Numerous stories used to be told of his precocity as a child, and of his smart sayings; sometimes of his generosity and sympathy with the poor and suffering. Now one is told he is somewhat of a pickle, but fables about royalty may always be received with more than a grain of salt. One of the stories told of him, which ought to be true, since it has the ring of childhood about

it, is well known. When a small boy, his Austrian governess, of whom he was very fond,
reproved him for using his knife in place of a
fork. "Gentlemen never do so," she said.
"But I am a King," he replied. "Kings, still
less, eat with their knives," said the governess.
"*This* King does," was the composed reply of the
child.

The etiquette of the Spanish Court, although it
was much modified by Alfonso XII., is still very
formal. A perfectly infinite number of *mayor-
domos, caballerizos, gentiles hombres de casa y boca,
ujieres, alabarderos, monteros,* aides-de-camp,
Grandes de España de servicio, ladies-in-waiting,
lackeys, servants, and attendants of every possible description abound. A man going to an
audience with royalty uncovers as he enters the
Palace. First, he will find the *alabardero de
servicio* placed at the entrance of the vestibule;
farther on, more *alabarderos.* Whenever a Grande
de España, a prelate, a grand cross, or a title of
Castiíe passes, these guards strike the marble
floor with their arms—a noise which may well
cause the uninitiated to start. Three halls are
used for grouping, according to their rank, those
who are about to be presented: first, the *saleta,*
where ordinary people—all the world, in fact—
wait; next, the *cámara,* for those who have titles
or wear the grand cross; third, the *antecámara,*
reserved for the Grandes of Spain, and *gentiles
hombres en ejercio.* The Grandes of Spain, cham-

berlains of the King, share between them the
service of his Majesty. They are called in rota-
tion, one day's notice being given before they are
expected to attend in the Palace. In the ante-
chamber of the King there is always the *Grande*
in waiting, the lady-in-waiting on the Queen, two
aides-de-camp, and a *gentil hombre del interio*
(the last must not be confounded with the *gentiles
hombres en ejercio*, who have the right to enter the
ante-chamber). There are, of course, equerries
(*caballerizos*) who attend, as ours do, on horseback, when the King or Queen goes out; but the
most essentially Spanish attendants are the Monteros de Espinosa, who have the exclusive right
to watch while Royalty sleeps. These attendants
must all be born in Espinosa; it is an hereditary
honour, and the wives of the existing Monteros
are careful to go to Espinosa when they expect an
addition to their family, as no one not actually
born there can hold the office. At the present
time this guard is recruited from captains or lieutenants on the retired list.

In the ante-chamber of each member of the
Royal Family two of these take their place at
eleven o'clock; they never speak, never sit down,
but pass the whole night pacing the room, crossing each other as they go, until morning relieves
them from what must be rather a trying watch.
At eleven o'clock each evening there is a solemn
procession of servants and officials in imposing
uniforms down the grand staircase of the Palace;

every door is closed and locked by a gentleman
wearing an antique costume and a three-cornered
hat, and having an enormous bunch of keys.
From that time the Palace remains under the exclusive charge of the Monteros de Espinosa. Although this is the official programme, it is to be
hoped the hour is not a fixed one. It would be a
little cruel to put the Royal Family to bed so
early, without regard to their feelings; especially
as Madrid is essentially a city of late hours, and
the various members of it would have to scamper
away from opera, or in fact any entertainment,
as if some malignant fairy were wanting to cast a
spell at the witching hour of midnight. There are
some curious superstitions, however, about being
abroad when the clocks strike twelve, which we
must suppose do not now affect the Madrileño.

While the old church of Atocha was still standing, the Court, with a royal escort, or what is
called *escadron de salut*, all the dignitaries of the
Palace in attendance, guards, outriders, etc., in
gorgeous array, drove in half state (*media gala*)
across Madrid and the *paseos* to hear the *salut*
"*sa'nt*" on Saturday. The Queen Regent and her
daughters, but not often the King, now visit in
turn some of the churches, but without the old
state or regularity.

Since the death of Alfonso XII. many of the
purely Spanish customs of the Court have been
modified or discontinued. Although the late
King was credited with a desire to reduce the

civil list, and to adopt more English customs, he was to some extent in the hands of the Conservatives, who had been the means of his restoration, and when he went forth to put an end to the Carlist insurrection and finish the civil war, which had laid desolate the Northern provinces and ruined commerce and industry for some seven years, it was at the head of a personal following of over five hundred people. Nor was the Court much, if any, less numerous when the Royal Family removed in the summer to the lovely Palace of St. Ildefonso at La Granja—that castle in the air, which has no equal in Europe, hanging, as it does, among gardens, forests, rivers, and lakes, three thousand eight hundred and forty feet above the level of the sea.

The Queen is Austrian, and she has never gone out of her way to conciliate the people by making herself really Spanish. This she has left to the Infanta Isabel, the eldest sister of Alfonso XII. For many years before the birth of her brother, the Infanta Isabel was Princess of Asturias, as heiress apparent of the Crown. With the advent of a boy, she became, of course, only Infanta, losing the rank which she had held up to this time. Being but a child at the time, she perhaps knew or cared little for any difference it may have made in her surroundings. She shared in the flight of the Royal Family to France in 1868, and her education was completed in Paris. When the whirligig of Spanish politics called her brother Alfonso, who at the time was a military student at Sandhurst, to the throne from which his mother had been driven, Princess Isabel returned with him to Madrid, and was once more installed in the Palace, above the Manzanares, as Princess of Asturias. This rank remained hers during the short episode of her brother's marriage to his cousin Mercédes, and the melancholy death of the girl Queen at the moment when a direct heir to the throne was expected. Once more, when the daughter of Alfonso's second wife, the present Queen Regent, was born, the Infanta Isabel became her title, and she took again the lower rank.

Nothing in history is more pathetic than this first marriage of Alfonso XII. and its unhappy termination. The children of Queen Isabel and those of her sister, the Duquesa de Montpensier, had been brought up together, and there was a boy-and-girl attachment between the Prince of Asturias and his cousin Mercédes. When Alfonso became King, almost as it seemed by accident, and it was thought necessary that he should marry, the boy gravely assured his Ministers that he was quite willing to do so, and in fact intended to marry his cousin. Nothing could be more inopportune, nothing more contrary to the welfare of the distracted country! From the time that the notorious "Spanish marriages" had become facts, the Duke of Montpensier had been an intriguer. The birth of heirs to the throne of Spain (it is useless to go back to those long-past scandals) had completely upset the machinations of Louis Philippe and his Ministers. So long as Don Francisco de Assis and the Spanish nation chose to acknowledge the children as legitimate, there was nothing to be done. The direct hope of seeing his sons Kings of Spain faded from the view of the French husband of the sister of Isabel II., but he never for one moment ceased to intrigue. Although loaded with benefits and kindness by the Queen, Montpensier took no small part in the revolution which drove her from the country. Topete, and Serrano — who had once been what the Spaniards called *Pollo Real* himself — were bound in honour to uphold his candidature for the vacant throne; their promise had been given long before the *pronunciamiento* at Cadiz had made successful revolution possible. Prim alone stood firm: "*Jamas, jamas !*" (Never, never!) he replied to every suggestion to bring Montpensier forward. In those words he signed his own death-warrant. His actual murderers were never brought to justice, ostensibly were never found; but there never was a Spaniard who doubted that the foul deed was the result of instigation.

To have Mercédes as Queen Consort, was to bring her father once more within the limits of practical interference with national politics. To all remonstrance, however, the young King had one answer: " I have promised," and the nation, recognising that as a perfectly valid argument, acquiesced, though with many forebodings. The marriage took place, and within a few months the girl Queen was carried with her unborn child to the melancholy Pantéon de los Principes at the Escorial.

The marriage of the Infanta Isabel with Count Girgenti, a Neapolitan Bourbon, was an unhappy one, and she obtained a legal separation from him after a very short matrimonial life. Spaniards have a perfect genius for giving apt nicknames. Scarcely was the arrangement for the marriage made known when the Count's name was changed to that of *Indecente*. He fought, however, for Isabel II. at Alcolea, which was at any rate acting more decently than did Montpensier, who had furnished large sums of money to promote the rising against his confiding sister-in-law, and, in fact, never ceased his machinations against every person and every thing that stood in his way, until death fortunately removed him from the arena of Spanish politics, his one overmastering ambition unfulfilled. He had neither managed to ascend the throne himself, nor see any of his children seated there, except for the few months that Mercédes, "beloved of the King and of the nation," shared the throne of Alfonso XII.

The Infanta Isabel, except for the episode of her exile in France, has always lived in the Royal Palace of Madrid, having her own quarters, and her little court about her. At times she has been the butt of much popular criticism, and even dislike, but she has outlived it all, and is now the most popular woman in Spain. It must have required no common qualities to have lived without discord—as a separated wife—with her brother and her younger sisters; then with Queen Mercédes, her cousin as well as sister-in-law; again, during the time of the King's widowhood and her own elevation to the rank of Princess of Asturias, and, finally, since the second marriage of her brother, and his untimely death, with Maria Cristina and her young nephew and nieces.

One thing is to be said in favour of Isabel II. Deprived of all ordinary education herself, as a part of the evil policy of her mother, she was careful that her own children should not have to complain of the same neglect. One and all have been thoroughly educated: the Infanta Paz, now married to a Bavarian Archduke, has shown considerable talent as a poetess; and the Infanta Isabel is universally acknowledged to be a clever and a cultivated woman, inheriting much of her mother's charm of manner, and noted for ready wit and quick repartee. Her popularity, as I have said, is great, for she is careful to keep up all the Spanish customs. She is constantly to be seen in public, and, above and beyond all things, she never fails in attendance at the bull-fight, wearing the white mantilla. This alone would cover a multitude of sins, supposing the Infanta to be credited with them; but there has never been a breath of scandal connected with her. She is very devout, and never fails in the correct religious duties and public appearances. At the fair, and on *Noche buena*, she fills her carriage with the cheap toys and sweetmeats which mean so much to Spanish children, and she must be a veritable fairy godmother to those who come within her circle. She takes a close personal interest in many sisterhoods and societies for the help of the poor. In a word, she is *muy simpática* and *muy Española*. What could one say more?

A gala procession in Madrid is something to be remembered, if it be only for the wealth of magnificent embroideries and fabrics displayed. The royal carriages are drawn by eight horses, having immense plumes of ostrich feathers, of the royal colours, yellow and red, on their heads, and gorgeous hangings of velvet, with massive gold embroideries reaching almost to the ground; the whole of the harness and trappings glitter with gold and silk. The grooms, leading each horse, are equally magnificently attired, their dresses being also one mass of needlework of gold on velvet. Equerries, outriders, and military guards precede and surround the royal carriages, and the cavalcade is lengthened by having a *coche de respecto*, caparisoned with equal splendour, following each one in which a royal person is being conveyed. Behind come the carriages of the Grandes, according to rank, all drawn by at least six horses, with trappings little, if at all, inferior

to those of the Court, and each with its enormous
plume of gaily-coloured ostrich feathers, showing
the livery of its owner. In addition to all this
grandeur, the balconies of the great houses lining
the route of the processions display priceless heirlooms of embroideries, hanging before each window from basement to roof. If these ancient
decorations could speak, what a strange story
they might tell of the processions they have seen
pass! In honour of the victories over the Moors;
of the heroes of the New World; of the miserable
murders of the *Autos-da-fé ;* of the entry of the
Rey absoluto, to inaugurate the " Terror," on to
the contemptible " galas " of Isabel II., supposed
to keep the people quiet; and, almost the last, the
entry of Alfonso XII., after he had put an end
to the Carlist war! On the day of rejoicing
for " La Gloriosa " there was no such display,
although all Madrid was *en fête*. It was the
triumph of the people, and their heirlooms do not
take the form of priceless embroideries.

In former days the receptions at the Palace
were known as *besamanos* (to kiss hand). On
Holy Thursday the Royal Family and all the
Court visit seven churches on foot—at least, that
is the correct number, though sometimes not
strictly adhered to. As no vehicular traffic is
allowed on that day or on Good Friday, the
streets where the royal procession pass are swept
and laid with fresh sand. The ladies are in gala
costume, and drag their trains behind them, all

wearing the national mantilla. All Madrid also visits its seven or less number of churches, passing without obeisance before the high altars, on which there is no Host,—as the people will tell you *su Majestad* is dead,—and after the *funcion* is over there is a general parade in the Puerta del Sol and the Carrera de San Geronimo, to show off the smart costumes of the ladies, while the officers sit in chairs outside the Government offices and smoke, admiring the prospect.

CHAPTER VII

POPULAR AMUSEMENTS

NOTHING strikes one so much in studying the popular customs and pleasures of Spain as the antiquity of them all. Constantly one finds one's self back in prehistoric times, and to date only from the days when Spain was a Roman province is almost modernity. No one can travel through Spain, or spend any time there, without becoming aware that, however many other forms of recreation there may be, two are universal and all-absorbing in their hold on the widely differing provinces — dancing and the bull-ring. In the Basque Provinces, the national game of *pelota*, a species of tennis, played without rackets, is still kept up, and is jealously cultivated in the larger towns, such as Vitoria, San Sebastian, and Bilbao. In Madrid at the present time it is played in large courts built on purpose, and attracts many strangers. To view it, however, as a national sport, one should see it in some of the mountain villages, where it is still the great recreation for Sundays and religious *fiestas*. The working-classes also play at throwing the hammer or

crowbar. This is more especially the case
in the Northern provinces, where the workmen
are a sound, healthy, and sober race, enjoying
simple and healthy amusements, and affording
an excellent example to those of countries considering themselves much more highly civilised.

Pigeon-shooting, which was a great favourite
with the late King Alfonso XII., and was made
fashionable among the aristocracy in Madrid by
him, is a very old sport—if it deserves the name
—among the Valencians. Near La Pechina, at
Valencia, where the great *tiro de las palomas* takes
place, was found, in 1759, an inscription: *Soda-
licium vernarum colentes Isid*. This, Ford tells us,
was an ancient *cofradiá* to Isis, which paid for
her *culto*. Cock-fighting is still practised in most
of the Spanish towns, as well as in Valencia, the
regular cock-pits being constantly frequented in
Madrid; but it is looked upon as suited only to
barrio's bajos, and is not much, if at all, patronised even by the middle classes. It is said by
those who have seen it to be particularly brutal;
but it was never a very humanising amusement
when practised by the English nobility not such
a very long time back.

Whatever amusements, however, may be popular in the towns, or in particular provinces, the guitar and the dance are universal. So much has been
written about the Spanish national dances that
an absurd idea prevails in England that they are
all very shocking and indecent. It is necessary,

however, to go very much out of one's way, and
to pay a good round sum, to witness those gypsy
dances which have come down unchanged from
the remotest ages.   As Ford truly says, "Their
character is completely Oriental, and analogous
to the *ghawarsee* of the Egyptians and the Hindoo
nautch."   "The well-known statue at Naples of
the Venere Callipige is the undoubted representa-
tion of a Cadiz dancing-girl, probably of Telethusa
herself."   These dances have nothing whatever
in common with the national dances as now to be
seen on the Spanish stage.   They are never performed except by gypsies, in their own quarter of
Seville, and are now generally gotten up as a
show for money.   Men passing through Seville go
to these performances, as an exhibition of what
delighted Martial and Horace, but they do not
generally discuss them afterwards with their lady
friends, and to describe one of these more than
doubtful dances as being performed by guests in
a Madrid drawing-room, as an English lady jour-
nalist did a short time ago in the pages of a
respectable paper, is one of those libels on Spain
which obtain currency here out of sheer ignorance of the country and the people.

Wherever two or three men and women of the
lower classes are to be seen together in Spain during their play-time, there is a guitar, with singing
and dancing.   The verses sung are innumerable
short stanzas by unknown authors; many, perhaps, improvised at the moment.   The *jota*, the

malaguena, and the *seguidilla* are combinations of music, song, and dance; the last two bear distinct indications of Oriental origin; each form is linked to a traditional air, with variations. The *malaguena* is Andalusian, and the *jota* is Aragonese; but both are popular in Castile. All are love-songs, most of them of great grace and beauty. Some writers complain that some of these dance-songs are coarse and more or less indecent; others aver that they never degenerate into coarseness. *Quien sabe?* Perhaps it is a case of *Honi soit qui mal y pense*. In any case, throughout the length and breadth of Spain, outside the wayside *venta*, or the barber's shop, in the *patios* of inns, or wherever holiday-makers congregate, there is the musician twanging his guitar, there are the dancers twirling about in obvious enjoyment to the accompaniment of the stamping, clapping, and encouraging cries of the onlookers, and the graceful little verse, with its probably weird and plaintive cadence:

> Era tan dichoso autes
> De encontrarte en mi canimo !
> Y, sin embargo, no siento
> El haberte conocido.

> I was so happy before
> I had met you on my way !
> And yet there is no regret
> That I have learned to know you.

The *malaguena* and the *seguidilla*, which is

more complicated, are generally seen on the stage
only in Madrid, where they must charm all who
can appreciate the poetry of motion.   The dance
of the peasant in Castile is always the *jota Aragonesa*.   The part the tambourine and the
castanets play in these dances must be seen and
heard to be understood: they punctuate not only
the music, but also the movement, the sentiment,
and the refrain.   The Andaluces excel in playing
on the castanets.   These are, according to Ford,
the "Baetican *crusmata* and *crotola* of the an-
cients": and *crotola* is still a Spanish term for the
tambourine.   Little children may be seen snap-
ping their fingers or clicking two bits of slate
together, in imitation of the castanet player; but
the continuous roll, or succession of quick taps, is
an art to be learned only by practice.   The castanets are made of ebony, and are generally
decorated with bunches of smart ribbons, which
play a great part in the dance.

The popular instrument in the Basque and
Northern provinces is the bagpipe, and the dances
are quite different from those of the other parts
of Spain.   The *zortico zorisco*, or "evolution of
eight," is danced to sound of tambourines, fifes,
and a kind of flageolet—*el silbato*, resembling the
rude instruments of the Roman Pifferari—probably of the same origin.

Theatrical representations have always been a
very popular form of recreation among the inhabitants of the Iberian continent, from the days

when the plays were acted by itinerant performers, "carrying all their properties in a sack, the
stage consisting of four wooden benches, covered
with rough boards, a blanket suspended at the
back, to afford a green-room, in which some
musician sang, without accompaniment, old ballads to enliven the proceedings." This is Cervantes's description of the national stage in the
time of his immediate predecessor, Lope de
Rueda.

The Spanish *zarzuela* appears to have been the
forerunner and origin of all musical farce and
"opera comique," only naturalised in our country
during the present generation. The theatres in
all the provinces are always full, always popular;
the pieces only run for short periods, a perpetual
variety being aimed at by the managers—a thing
easily to be understood when one remembers
that the same audience, at any rate in the boxes
and stalls, frequent them week in, week out.
In Madrid, with a population of five hundred
thousand inhabitants, there are nineteen theatres.
With the exception of the first-class theatres, the
people pay two *reales* (5*d.*) for each small act or
piece, and the audience changes many times during the evening, a constant stream coming and
going. Long habit and familiarity with good
models have made the lower class of playgoers
critical; their judgment of a piece, or of an actor,
is always good and worth having.

The religious *fiestas* must also count among the

amusements of the people in Spain. Whether it be the Holy Week in Seville or Toledo, the *Romeria* of Santiago, the *Veladas*, or vigils, of the great festivals, or the day of Corpus Christi, which takes place on the first Thursday after Trinity Sunday—at all these the people turn out in thousands, dressed in their smartest finery, and combine thorough enjoyment with the performance of what they believe to be a religious duty. There is little or no drunkenness at these open-air festivities, but much gaiety, laughter, fluttering of fans, "throwing of sparks" from mischievous or languishing eyes—and at the end always a bull-fight.

Here we touch the very soul of Spain. Take away the bull-rings, make an end of the *toreros*, and Spain is no longer Spain—perhaps a country counting more highly in the evolution of humanity as a whole, but it will need another name if that day ever comes, of which there does not now seem to be the remotest possibility. All that can be said is that to-day there is a party, or there are individuals, in the country who profess to abhor the bull-fight, and wish to see it ended; it is doubtful if up to this time any Spaniard ever entertained such an "outlandish" notion. The bull-fight is said to have been founded by the Moors of Spain, although bulls were probably fought with or killed in Roman amphitheatres. The principle on which they were founded was the display of horsemanship, use of the lance, courage,

coolness, and dexterity—all accomplishments of
the Arabs of the desert. It is undoubtedly the
latter qualities which make the sport so fascinating
to English *aficionados*, of whom there are many,
and have caused the *fiestas de toros* to live on in
the affections of the whole Spanish people. In its
earliest days, gentlemen, armed only with the
rejon, the short spear of the original Iberian,
about four feet long, fought in the arena with the
bulls, and it was always a fair trial of skill and a
display of good horsemanship.

When the fatal race of the French Bourbons
came to the throne, and the country was inundated
with foreign favourites, the Court and the French
hangers-on of the kings turned the fashion away
from the national sport, and it gradually fell into
the hands of the lower classes, professional bull-
fighters taking the place of the courtly players of
old, and these were drawn from the lowest and
worst ranks of the masses; the sporting element,
to a great extent, died out, and the whole spectacle became brutalised. *Pan y toros* (bread and
bulls) were all the people wanted, and, crushed
out of all manliness by their rulers, and taught a
thirst for cruelty and bloodshed by the example
of their religious *autos-da-fé*, the bull-fight became the revolting spectacle which foreigners—
especially the English—have been so ready to
rail against as a disgrace to the Spanish nation,
while they rarely let an opportunity escape
them of assisting as interested spectators at what

they condemned so loudly, and they quite forgot their own prize-ring, and other amusements equally brutal and disgraceful. If the *corrida de toros* was ever as bad as it has been described by some, it has improved very much of late years, and most of its revolting features are eliminated. The pack of dogs, which used to be brought in when a bull was dangerous to the human fighters, has long been done away with. The *media luna*, which we are told was identical with the instrument mentioned in *Joshua*, is no longer tolerated to hamstring the unfortunate bull; and if a horse is gored in the fair fight, there are men especially in attendance to put him out of his misery at once. It is doubtful whether the animal suffers more than, or as much as, the unhappy favourites, that are sent alive, and in extremest torture, to Amsterdam and other foreign cities, to be manufactured into essence of meat and such-like dainties, after a life of cruelly hard work in our omnibuses and cabs has made them no longer of use as draught animals.

The bull-fighter of to-day is by no means drawn from the dregs of the people; there is, at any rate, one instance of a man of good birth and education attaining celebrity as a professional *torero*. He risks his life at every point of the conflict, and it is his coolness, his courage, his dexterity in giving the *coup de grâce* so as to cause no suffering, that raise the audience to such a pitch of frenzied excitement. I speak wholly from hearsay, for I have myself only witnessed a *corrida de novillos*—in which the bulls are never killed, and have cushions fixed on their horns— and a curious fight between a bull and an elephant, who might have been described as an " old campaigner," in which there was no bloodshed, and much amusement. My sympathies always went with the bull,—who, at least, was not consulted in the matter of the fight,—as I have seen the popular *espada*, with his own particular *chulo*, a mass of white satin and gold embroidery, driving out to the bull-ring on the afternoon of a *fiesta*, bowing with right royal grace and dignity to the plaudits of the people. I was even accused of having given the evil eye to one well-known favourite as he passed my balcony, when I wished, almost audibly, that the bull might have his turn for once in a way that afternoon. And he had; for the popular *espada* was carried out of the ring apparently dead, the spectators came back looking white and sick, and I felt like a very murderess until I learned later that he was not dead. All Madrid, almost literally, called to inquire for him daily, filling books of signatures, as if he had been an emperor at least. Personally, I was more interested in his courage after the event and the devotion of his *chulo*, who never left his side, but held his hands while the injured leg was cut off, in three separate operations, without any anæsthetic. Eventually, he completely recovered, and was fitted with an admirable mechanical cork limb in place of the one removed in three detachments; and my sense of evil responsibility was quite removed when I heard that his young wife was delighted to think that he could never enter the bull-ring as a fighter again, and her anxieties were at an end.

It is quite impossible to over-estimate the popularity of the *toreros* with the Spanish people. They are the friends and favourites of the aristocracy, the demi-gods of the populace. You never see one of them in the streets without an admiring circle of worshippers, who hang on every word and gesture of the great man; and this is no cult of the hour, it is unceasing. They are always known for their generosity, not only to injured comrades, but to any of the poor in need. Is there a disaster by which many are injured—flood, tempest, or railway accident? Immediately a bull-fight is arranged for the sufferers, and the whole *cuadrilla* will give their earnings to the cause. Not only so, but the private charities of these popular favourites are immense, and quite unheard of by the public. They adopt orphans, pay regular incomes to widows, as mere parts of every-day work. They are, one and all, religious men; the last thing they do, before entering the arena with their life in their hands, is to confess and receive absolution in the little chapel in the Bull-Ring, spending some time in silent prayer before the altar, while the wife at home is burning candles to the Virgin, and offering her prayers for his safety during the whole time that the *corrida* lasts. Extreme unction is always in readiness, in case of serious accident to the *torero*, the priest (*mufti*) slipping into the chapel before the public arrive on the scene.

Rafael Molina Lagartijo, one of the veterans of the bull-fighters, and an extreme favourite with the people for many years, died recently, after living for some time in comparative retirement in his native Córdoba. Some idea of the important place which these men occupy in Spanish society may be gathered from the numerous notices which appeared in the newspapers of all shades of political opinion after his death. I quote from the article which appeared in the charming little illustrated *Blanco y Negro*, of Madrid, on the favourite of the Spanish public. In what, to us, seems somewhat inflated language, but which is, however, quite simple and natural to the Spaniard, the writer began his notice thus:

" He who has heard the magic oratory of Castelar, has listened to the singing of Gayarre, the declamation of Cabro, has read Zorilla, and witnessed the *torear* of Lagartijo, may say, without any kind of reservation, that there is nothing left for him to admire! " Having thus placed the popular bull-fighter on a level with orators, authors, and musicians of the first rank, the writer goes on to describe the beauties of Lagartijo's play in words which are too purely technical of the ring to make translation possible, and adds:

" He who has not seen the great *torero* of Córdoba
in the plenitude of his power will assu   not
comprehend why the name of Lagartijo for more
than twenty years filled *plazas* and playbills, nor
why the *aficionados* of to-day recall, in speaking
of his death, times which can never be surpassed.
. . . The *toreo* (play) of Lagartijo was always
distinguished by its classic grace, its dignity and
consummate art, the absence of affectation, or
struggle for effect.   In every part of the fight the
figure of Rafael fell naturally into the most graceful attitudes; and for this reason he has always
worn the rich dress of the *torero* with the best
effect.   He was the perfect and characteristic type
of a *torero*, such as Spanish fancy has always imagined it.   Lagartijo died with his eyes fixed on
the image of the Virgen de los Dolores, to whom
he had always confidently committed his life of
peril, and with the dignity and resignation of a
good man."

The article was illustrated with numerous portraits of Don Rafael: in full *torero* dress in 1886;
his very last photograph; views of him in the
courtyard of his home in Córdoba, and outside
the Venta San Rafael, where he took his coffee
in the evening, and others.   The notice concludes
by saying that his life was completely dedicated
to his property, which he managed himself, and
he was looked upon as the guardian angel of the
labourers on his farm.   *Probre Rafael !*   " The
lovers of the bull-fight are lamenting the death

of the *torero*, but the poor of Córdoba mourn the loss of their 'Señor Rafael.' "

The wives of the *toreros* are generally celebrated for their beauty, their wit, and their devotion to their husbands—indeed, the men have a large choice before them when choosing their helpmates for life. To their wives is due much of the making and all the keeping up of the elaborate and costly dress of the *torero*. They are, as someone has said, " ferociously virtuous," and share in the open-handed generosity of their husbands. The earnings of a successful *torero* are very large. In some cases, they make as much as £4000 or £5000 a year of English money, during the height of their popularity, and retire to end their days in their native and beloved Andalucia.

Whatever may be said by foreigners of the brutalising effect of the Spanish popular game, it certainly has no more effect on those who witness or practise it than fox-hunting has on Englishmen, and it is doubtful whether there is any more cruelty in one sport than in the other. The foxes are fostered and brought up for the sole purpose of being harried to death, without even a semblance of fair play being allowed to them, and if a fox-hunter risks his life it is only as a bad rider that he does so. There is no danger and certainly no dignity in the English sport, even if it indirectly keeps up the breed of horses.

A curious incident is related by Count Vasili as having happened in the Bull-Ring in Madrid some years ago during a *corrida* of Cúchares, the celebrated *espada*. It is usual during *fiestas* of charity to enclose live sparrows in the *banderillas* which it is part of the play to affix, at great risk to the *torero*, in the shoulders of the bull; the paper envelope bursts, and the birds are set at liberty. Crossing the arena, one of the men carelessly hit at a bird turning wildly about in its efforts to escape, and killed it. "In my life," says the Count, "I have never seen such a spectacle. Ten thousand spectators, standing up, wildly gesticulating, shouting for death on the 'cruel *torero*'; nay, some even threw themselves into the arena, ready to lynch the heartless creature!"

Horse-racing may now be said to have been fairly established in Spain in most of the great centres, and the Hippodrome in Madrid is little behind one of England's popular race-courses in its crowds, the brilliant dresses of the ladies, and the enthusiasm evoked; but whether it will ever supersede the really national *fiesta* is to be doubted. The upper classes also affect polo, tennis, and croquet, and go in a good deal for gymnastics, fencing, and fives.

Cycling does not appear to commend itself greatly to the Spanish idea of recreation. Bicycles are, of course, to be seen in the large and more modern towns, but they are never very numerous, and as far as ladies are concerned, may be said to have made no way.

I have referred to a curious spectacle several times presented in Madrid, chiefly in *fiestas* for charitable purposes, where an elephant was introduced into the Bull-Ring to fight, in place of the usual *cuadrilla* of men. This was an old elephant named Pizarro, a great favourite of many years' standing with the Madrileños. He was an enormous animal, but one of his tusks had been broken off about a third from the tip, so that he had only one to use in warfare or as protection. He was tethered in the centre of the arena, by one of his hind legs, to a stump about twelve inches high. Then the bulls were let out one at a time. Meanwhile, Pizarro was amusing himself by eating oranges which were showered on him by his admirers on the benches. With the greatest coolness he continued his repast, picking up orange after orange with his trunk, all that he was careful to do being to keep his face to the bull, turning slowly as his enemy galloped round the ring trying to take him in flank. At last the bull prepared to charge; Pizarro packed away his trunk between his tusks, and quietly waited the onslaught. The bull rushed at him furiously; but the huge animal, quite good-naturedly and a little with the air of pitying contempt, simply turned aside the attack with his one complete horn, and as soon as the bull withdrew, a little nonplussed, went on picking up and eating his oranges as before. Bull after bull gave up the contest as impossible, and contentedly went out between the *cabestros* sent in to fetch them.   At last one more persistent or courageous than the others came bounding in.   Pizarro realised at once that for the moment he must pause in eating his dessert; but he became aware at the same time that in turning round to face the successive bulls, he had gradually wound himself up close to the stump, and had no room to back so as to receive the attack.   The most interesting incident in the whole affray was to watch the elephant find out, by swinging his tethered leg, first in one direction and then in another, how to free himself.   This he did, first by swinging his leg round and round over the stump, then by walking slowly round and round, always facing the bull, and drawing his cord farther and farther until he was perfectly free: then he was careful only to turn as on a pivot, keeping the rope at a stretch. Finally the bull charged at him with great fury; stepping slightly aside, Pizarro caught him up sideways on his tusks, and held him up in the air, perfectly impotent and mad with rage.   When he considered the puny creature had been sufficiently shown his inferiority, he gently put him down, and the astonished and humbled bull declined further contest.   The fighting bulls of Spain are wonderfully small in comparison with English animals, it should be said.

Every night, after his turn at the circus was over poor old Pizarro used to walk home alone under my balcony, open his stable door with his own latch-key, or at least his trunk, and put himself to bed like any Christian.

One of the most fashionable amusements in Madrid is to attend on the morning of the bull-fight while the *espadas* choose the particular bulls they wish to have as enemy, and affix their colours, the large rosette of ribbon which shows which of the *toreros* the bull is to meet in deadly conflict. The bulls are then placed in their iron cages in the order in which they are to enter the arena. The fashionable ladies and other *aficionados* of the sport then drive back to Madrid to luncheon and to prepare for the entertainment of the afternoon.

CHAPTER VIII

THE PRESS AND ITS LEADERS

PERHAPS there are few countries where the influence of the Press is greater than in Spain, and this is largely due to the fact that while the journals are read by everyone, for a great number of the people they form the only literature. The free library is not yet universal in the country, though, doubtless, in the near future it may become general. In the meantime, every imaginable shade of political opinion has its organ; even the Bull-Ring has at least two excellently illustrated newspapers; and the extra sheets, printed hastily and sold immediately after the *corrida* has terminated, have an enormous sale. Deserving of mention is the curious little paper known as the " Night-cap of Madrid," because it is supposed to be impossible for anyone to go to rest until he has read the late edition, which comes out not long before midnight. It is said to have no politics, and only pretends to give all the news of the world. There are many illustrated papers, both comic and serious. The charmingly artistic little *Blanco y Negro*, beauti-

9

fully gotten up, is at the head of all the more dignified illustrated journals of the country.   There
are no kiosks; the papers are sold by children
or by old women in the streets, and the Madrid
night is rent by the appalling cries of these itinerant vendors of literature.   For the Spanish newspaper is always literature, which is a good deal
more than can be said for some of the English
halfpenny Press.   Whatever may be the politics
of the particular journal, its *Castellano* is perfect;
perhaps a little stilted or pompous, but always
dignified and well-written.

The journalists of Madrid have a special facility
for saying with an air of extreme innocence what
they, for various reasons, do not care to express
quite openly.   Allegories, little romances, stories
of fact full of clever words of " double sense " make
known to the initiated, or those who know how to
read between the lines, much that might otherwise awaken the disagreeable notice of the censor,
when there is one.   There is an air of good-
natured raillery which takes off the edge of political rancour, and keeps up the amenities and the
dignity of the Spanish Press.   Only the other
day one of the leading English journals pointed
out what a dignified part the Press of Madrid, of
every shade of politics, had played in the recent
effort made by some foreign newspapers—of a
class which so far does not exist in Spain—to
make mischief and awaken national jealousy between England and Spain on the subject of the

works now being carried out by the English
Government at Gibraltar. The Spanish newspapers, of all shades of opinion, have made it
abundantly evident that their country entertains
no unworthy suspicion of England's good faith,
and has not the smallest intention of being led
into strained or otherwise than perfectly friendly
relations with their old allies of the Peninsular
War, to gratify the rabid enmity of a section of a
Press foreign to both countries. This is, perhaps,
the more remarkable because a certain amount
of misunderstanding of England exists among
some elements of the Spanish Press.

The Liberal party in Spain is, in fact, the party
of progress, and the nation has at last awakened
from its condition of slavery under unworthy
rulers, and is practically united in its determination to return to its place among the nations of
Europe.

There are many shades of Liberalism, and even
Republicanism, but, as will be seen in another
place, the real welfare of the people, and not the
success of a mere political party, is the underlying
motive of all, however wild and unpractical may
be some of the dreams for the carrying out of
these ideas of universal progress. It is impossible
for a Spaniard to conceive of maligning or be-
littling his own country for merely party purposes;
and, therefore, when he finds an English newspaper calling itself " Liberal " he imagines the
word to have the same signification it has in his

own country. So it has come to pass that many
of the worst misrepresentations—to use a very
mild term—of a portion of the English Press have
been reproduced in Spanish newspapers, and believed by their readers.

Among the principal newspapers, in a crowd of
less important ones, *La Época*, Conservative
and dynastic ranks first; this is the journal of the
aristocrats, of the " upper ten thousand," or those
who aspire to be so, and it ranks as the *doyen* of
the whole Press. Its circulation is not so large as
that of some of the other papers, but its clientèle
is supposed to be of the best. *El Nacional* is also
Conservative, but belonging to the party of
Romero Robledo. What the exact politics of
that variation of Conservatism might be, it is
difficult, I might almost say impossible, for a
stranger to say. If you were told nothing about
it, and took it up accidentally to read of current
events, you would certainly suppose it to be independent, with a decidedly Liberal tendency. Still
it calls itself Conservative.

El Correo is Liberal, of the special type of
Sagasta, the present Prime Minister. *El Español*,
which also gives one the impression of independence, is Liberal after the manner of Gemaro.
El Heraldo, calling itself *Diario Independente*, is
credited with being the Liberal organ of Canal-
ijas. *El Liberal* and *El Pais* are Republican, and
El Correo Español is Carlist, or clerical. This
paper appears to be looked upon a good deal in

the nature of a joke by its colleagues, and quotations from it are always accompanied by notes of exclamation.

La Correspondéncia de España is a paper all by itself, an invention of Spanish journalism, and its unprecedented success is due to many of its quite unique peculiarities. Its originator, now a millionaire, is proud of relating that he arrived in Madrid with two dollars in his pocket. He it was who conceived the brilliant idea of founding a journal which should be the special organ of all. *"Diario politico independiente, y de noticias : Eco imparcial de la opinion y de la prensa,"* he calls it, and the fourth page, devoted to advertisements, would make the fortune of ten others. His boast was that it had no editor, paid no writers, and employed no correspondents. It simply possessed a certain number of " caterers " for news, who thrust themselves everywhere, picking up morsels of news—good, bad, and indifferent, for the most part scribbled in pencil and thrown into a receptacle from which they are drawn in any order, or none, and handed to the printer as " copy "; coming out in short, detached paragraphs of uneven length, ranging from three lines to twenty. Extracts from foreign newspapers, official news, provincial reports, money matters, religious announcements, accidents, everything comes out pell-mell—absolutely all " the voices of the flying day," in Madrid and everywhere else, in one jumble, without order or sequence, one paragraph frequently being a direct contradiction to another in the same sheet. There are three editions during the day, but the " Night-cap," which sums up them all, appears about ten o'clock or later, and it is scarcely an exaggeration to say that it is bought by almost every householder in the city.

The nature of the *Correspondéncia* has changed very little since its earliest days. It is a little more dignified, condescends even to short articles on current subjects of interest, but it is the same universal provider of news and gossip as ever. It goes with the times; so far as it has any leanings at all, it is with the Government of the hour; but it is for the most part quite impersonal, and it makes itself agreeable to all parties alike. Santa Ana, the clever initiator of this new and highly successful adventure in journalism, has two other very prosperous commercial enterprises in his hands — the manufacture of paper for printing and the supply of natural flowers. He himself is an enormous and indefatigable worker, personally looks after his various businesses, especially the *Correspondéncia*, and, mindful of his own early difficulties, he has created benefit societies for his workmen.

He who, being a foreigner, would attempt to understand Spanish politics, deserves to be classed with the bravest leaders of forlorn hopes. In the first place, it is doubtful whether Spaniards understand them themselves, although they talk, for the most part, of nothing else—except bulls.

Whenever and wherever two or three men or boys are gathered together, you may be quite certain as to the subject of their conversation— that is, if they show signs of excitement and interest in the matter under discussion. Each man you meet gives you the whole matter in a nutshell: he has studied politics ever since he was able to talk; all the other innumerable parties besides his own are *nada!* he can tell you exactly what is wrong with his country, and, what is more, exactly how it may all be made right. The only thing which puzzles one is that all the nutshells are different, and, as there are an unlimited number of them, all that one carefully learns today has to be as carefully unlearned to-morrow, and a fresh adjustment made of one's political spectacles. After all, however, this is very much what would happen in any country if we were in turn to sit at the feet of successive teachers, and try to bring their doctrines into any kind of accord. The peculiarity in Spain lies rather in the multiplicity of private political opinions and the energy with which they are expressed, and in the fact that they are all honest.

Emerson has somewhere said that "inconsistency is the bugbear of little minds." The Spanish politician has evidently not a little mind, for he has no fear whatever of inconsistency, nor, in fact, of making a *volte-face* whenever he sees any reason for doing so. There are Conservatives, Liberals, Republicans, Radicals, Socialists, as in other countries, but there are, besides all these, an infinite number of shades and tones of each political belief, each represented, as we have seen, by a newspaper of its own, and, for the most part, bearing the name of one man. It would seem, then, that you have only to make yourself acquainted with the opinions, or rather with the political acts, of that one man, and there you are! Vain and fond fancy! He has been a rabid Republican, perhaps, or he has belonged, at least, to the party which put up in Madrid in conspicuous letters, "The bastard race of the Bourbons is for ever fallen. Fit punishment of their obstinacy!" but you will find him to-day lending all the force of his paper to the support of the Queen Regent, and at the same time allying himself with the various classes of Republicans, even to the followers of Zorilla, who have, at any rate till now, been consistent enemies and haters of the Bourbon.

Señor Don Romero Robledo, one among the politicians of the day who possess the gift of perfect oratory, so common among his countrymen, is an example of this puzzling "open mind." He appeared first in the character of revolutionist in 1868; then he became the Minister of the Interior in Amadeo's short reign, held somewhat aloof from the wild experiment in a republic of Castelar, joined the party of Don Alfonso on the eve of its success, and supported Cánovas del Castillo in his somewhat retrograde policy in the restoration

of the very Bourbon whom he had announced as
"banished for ever," and, in fact, by his admirable
genius for organising his party, enabled the Government of Cánovas to continue to exist.   It is
said of him that he " buys men as one would buy
sheep," and that he will serve any cause so long
as he has the management of it, or rather so long
as he may pull the wires.   Comte Vasili says of
him: "In politics, especially Conservative politics,
men like Romero Robledo are necessary, finding
easily that ' the end justifies the means,' energetic, ambitious, always in the breach opposing
their qualities to the invasions of the parties of
extremes."   This was written of him some fifteen
years ago by one eminently qualified to judge.
At the present moment we find Señor Romero
Robledo refusing office, but consulted by the
Queen Regent in every difficulty.   In the late
crisis, when the Conservative party under Silvela,
called into office for the sake of carrying the extremely unpopular marriage of the Princess of
Asturias with the Count of Caserta, had nearly
managed to wreck the monarchy, or, at any rate,
the regency, and to bring the always dangerous
clerical question to an acute stage by suspending
the constitutional guarantees over the whole of
Spain, it was Romero Robledo who told the Queen
quite plainly that before anything else could be
done the guarantees must be restored, that the
liberties of the people could not be interfered
with, and that, in short, the Liberal party must

be called into office. Then we find him holding
meetings in which Conservatives, Republicans,
even Zorillistas, all combined, enthusiastically declaring that they are on the side of order and
progress, agreeing to hold up England, under her
constitutional monarch, as the most really democratic and free of all nations, since in no other
country, republican or otherwise, is the government, as a matter of fact, so entirely in the hands
of the people; swearing eternal enmity against
the interference of the clergy in government or
in education, but counselling " quiet determination without rancour or bigotry in dealing with
those of the clergy who openly, or through the
confessional, attempt to usurp authority which
it is intended they shall never again acquire in
Spain." In fact, to read Señor Romero Robledo's
discourses on these occasions, and the excellent
articles in the newspaper which represents his
views, *El Nacional*, one would imagine the Golden
Age to have dawned for Spain. Liberty, honour,
real religion, progress in science, art, manufactures, trade, the purification of politics, the ideal
of good government—these are only a few of the
things to which this amalgamation of parties is
solemnly pledged.

One thing, at least, is promising among so
much that might be put down as "words, words":
a general agreement as to the wisdom of making
the best of the present situation, opposing a firm
resistance to any attempt at a return to absolut-

ism on the part of the monarchy, or domination in temporal matters by the Church; but no change, no more *pronunciamientos*, no more civil wars. Whenever the political parties of a country merge their differences of opinion in one common cause, the end may be foreseen. This was what happened in 1868; and if the party of Romero Robledo is what it represents itself to be and holds together, we may hope to see the reign of the young Alfonso XIII. open with good auguries this year (1902), as it seems to be certain that he is to attain his majority two years in advance of the usual time.

The life, political career, and retirement of Emilio Castelar is one of the most pathetic pictures in history, and one altogether Spanish in character. It was after Amadeo had thrown down his crown, exclaiming, "A son of Savoy does not wear a crown on sufferance!" that the small party of Republicans—which Prim had said did not exist, and which had in fact only become a party at all during the disastrous period of uncertainty between the expulsion of Isabel II. and the election of the Italian prince—edged its way to the front, and Castelar became the head of something much worse than a paper constitution —a republic of visionaries. Don Quijote de la Mancha himself could scarcely have made a more pure-intentioned yet more unpractical President. Castelar, with his honest, unsophisticated opinions and theories, his unexampled oratory, which is said to have carried away crowds of men who did not understand or hear a word that he said, with the rhythm of his language, the simple majesty and beauty of his delivery, launched the nation into a government that might have been suited to the angels in heaven, or to what the denizens of this earth may become in far distant æons of evolution—a republic of dreams, headed by a dreamer. The awakening was rude, but it was efficient. When Castelar found that in place of establishing a millennium of peace and universal prosperity, he had let loose over the land all the elements of disorder and of evil, he had the greatness to acknowledge himself mistaken: his own reputation never troubled him, and he admitted that the Cortes, from which he had hoped so much, worked evil, not good. It is said that he himself called on General Pavía, the Captain-General of Madrid, to clear them out. The deputies—Castelar had withdrawn—sat firm: " Death rather than surrender," they cried. Pavía, however, ordered his men to fire once down the empty lobbies, and the hint was enough: the Cortes dispersed, and Pavía, had he so minded it, might have been military dictator of Spain. But he had no such ambition, though there were not wanting those who ascribed it to him.

As for Castelar, when angrily charged with inconsistency, he said: " Charge me with inconsistency, if you please. I will not defend myself. Have I the right to prefer my own reputation to the safety of my country? Let my name perish, let posterity pronounce its anathema against me, let my contemporaries send me into exile! Little care I! I have lived long enough! But let not the Republic perish through my weaknesses, and, above all, let no one say that Spain has perished in our hands!" Castelar went back to his chair of philosophy, which he had never resigned, poor as he left it, to the modest home and the devoted sister whom he loved so well — and no one laughed! Is there really any other country than Spain where such things can happen? His enthusiasm, his high-mindedness, his failures, his brave acknowledgment that he had failed, were accepted by the country in the exact spirit in which he had offered himself to her service, and the memory of Castelar stands as high to-day as ever it did in the respectful admiration of his fellow-countrymen.

CHAPTER IX

POLITICAL GOVERNMENT

THE Government of Spain ever since the restoration of Don Alfonso XII. has been in reality what it was only in name before—a constitutional monarchy. During the first years of the young King's reign, Cánovas del Castillo being Prime Minister, there was a distinctly reactionary tendency from the Liberalism of Prim and the revolutionary party of 1868. It was almost impossible that it should be otherwise, considering the wild tumult of the varying opinions and the experiments in government that the country had passed through; and some of the difficulties of the situation to-day are no doubt due to the concessions made to the ultra-Conservative party in the re-introduction of the religious orders, which had been suppressed during the regency of Cristina, and had never been tolerated even during the reign of the *piadosa*, Isabel II.

Prim had, from the first moment that the success of the Revolution was assured and the Queen and her *camarilla* had crossed the frontier to seek asylum in France, declared for a constitutional monarchy. "How can you have a monarchy without a king?" he was asked by Castelar. "How can you have a republic without republicans!" was his reply. He might have made himself king or military dictator, but he wanted to be neither; nor would he hear of Montpensier, to whom Topete and Serrano had pledged themselves.

The House of Savoy was the next heir to the Spanish throne, had the Bourbons become extinct, and to it the first glances of the Spanish king-maker were directed, but difficulties arose from the dislike of the Duke of Aosta himself to the scheme. A prince of some Liberal country was what was wanted: there was even some talk of offering the crown to the English Duke of Edinburgh, while one party dreamed of an Iberian amalgamation, and suggested Dom Luis of Portugal or his father Dom Ferdinand, the former regent. The candidature of Prince Leopold of Hohenzollern-Sigmaringen, who was a Roman Catholic, was looked upon with a certain amount of favour, but at the eleventh hour Napoleon III. made this scheme a pretext for the quarrel with Prussia which led to the fateful war of 1870 and 1871. Eventually, almost two years after the outbreak of the Revolution, Amadeo of Savoy was chosen by the Cortes at Madrid by a majority of one hundred and five votes, only twenty-three being given for Montpensier and sixty-three for a republic.

On the day that King Amadeo set foot on Spanish soil Prim was assassinated; it was perfectly well known at whose instigation, and the man whom the Spaniards themselves said was *demasiado honesto* (too honourable) for the hotchpotch of political parties into which he was thrown without a friend or helper, began his vain effort to rule a foreign nation in a constitutional manner. After he had thrown up the thankless task in despair, the absurd Republic of Zorilla and Castelar made confusion worse confounded, and it was with a feeling of relief to all that the *pronunciamiento* of Martinez Campos at Muviedro put an end to the Spanish Republic under Serrano, and proclaimed the son of Isabel II. as King.

He was but a lad of seventeen, but he had been educated in England; he was known to be brave, dignified, and extremely liberal, so that he was acclaimed throughout Spain, and during his short life he fully justified the high opinion formed of him. But the Government of Cánovas was reactionary, and when the unexpected death of Alfonzo XII. left his young wife, the present Maria Cristina of Austria, a widow under exceptionally trying circumstances, Cánovas himself placed his resignation in her hands, knowing that the Liberals were the party of the nation, and promised to give his own best efforts to work with what had up to then been his Opposition, for the good of the country and of the expected child, who a few months later had the unusual experience of being " born a king."

Whatever may be said about the present Regent, —though in truth little but good has been said or thought of her,—she has been most loyal to the constitution, holding herself absolutely aloof from all favouritism or even apparent predilection. She has devoted her life to the education of her son and to his physical well-being, for he was not a strong child in his early years, and she has done her best, possibly more than any but a woman could have done, to keep the ship of State not only afloat, but making headway during the minority of her son.

Two things militate against good government in Spain, and will continue to do so until the whole system is changed: what is known in the country as *caciquismo*, and the pernicious custom of changing all the Government officials, down to the very porter at the doors, with every change of ministry. It is much, however, that the Government does go out in a constitutional manner instead of by a military *pronunciamiento* on each occasion, as in the old days; also that a civilian and not a soldier is always at the head of it. In reality, there are two great parties in Madrid, and only two: the *Empleados* and the *Cesantes*— in plain English, the " Ins " and the " Outs." Whatever ministry is in power has behind it an immense army of provincial governors, secretaries, clerks, down to the porters, and probably even the charwomen who clean out the Government offices. This state of things is repeated over the whole country, and there is naturally created and sustained an enormous amount of bribery and corruption, which is continually at work discrediting all governments and giving to Spanish affairs that "bad name" which, according to our old proverb, is as bad as hanging. The *Cesantes* haunt certain *cafés* and possess certain newspapers, and the *Empleados* other *cafés* and other papers. The "Outs" and the "Ins" meet at night to discuss their prospects, and wonderful are the stories invented at these reunions, some of which even find their way into English newspapers—if their correspondents are not up to the ways of Spain—for we read ludicrous accounts of things supposed to have been taking place, and are treated to solemn prophecies of events never likely to occur, even in first-class English journals. It is naturally the interest of these subordinate employees of a vicious system to hasten or retard the day that shall see their respective chiefs change position, and if a few plausible untruths can do it, be assured they will not be wanting. Both in the popular novels, *de costumbres*, and in actual life, it is the commonest thing to hear a man described as a *Cesante*, in the same way that we should speak of him as being an engineer or a doctor, as if being out of place were just as much an employment as any other.

One thing that appears strange to a foreigner

about these *Cesantes* is that they never seem even to dream of seeking other employment; they simply sit down to wait until their particular patron is " in " again, and in the old days they were a constant force making for the *pronunciamiento* which would sooner or later make a place for them. As they had no means of existence except when in receipt of Government pay, it is easy to understand that, according to their views, they had to prepare for the evil day which assuredly awaited them, by appropriating and exacting all the money that was possible during their short reign of power. Probably the only difference between the highest and the lowest official was in the actual amount he was able to acquire when he was " in."

This system, subversive of all efficient service, and leading inevitably to the worst evils of misappropriation of the national funds, had perhaps its worst aspects in the colonies. A Government berth in Cuba was a recognised means of making a fortune, or of rehabilitating a man who had ruined himself by gambling at home. Appointments were made, not because the man was fitted for the post, but because he had influence—frequently that of some lady—with the person with whom the appointments lay, or because he was in need of an opportunity for making money easily. That there have always been statesmen and subordinate officials above all such self-seeking, men of punctilious honour and of absolutely clean hands, is known to all; but such men—as Espartero, for instance—too often threw up the sponge, and would have naught to do with governing nor with office of any description. Espartero, who is generally spoken of as the "Aristides of Spain," when living in his self-sought retirement at Logroño, even refused to be proclaimed as King during the days when the crown was going a-begging, though he would probably have been acclaimed as the saviour of his country by a large majority. Long years of foreign kings and their generally contemptible favourites and ministers, long years of tyranny and corruption in high places, leavened the whole mass of Spanish bureaucracy; but the heart of the nation remained sound, and those who would understand Spain must draw a distinct line between her professional place-hunters and her people.

Caciqueism is a mere consequence or outcome from the state of affairs already described. While the deputies to the Cortes are supposed to be freely elected as representatives by the people, in reality they are simply nominees of the heads of the two political powers which have been see-sawing as ministers for the last sixteen years. Two men since the assassination of Cánovas have alternately occupied the post of First Minister of the Crown: Don Práxadis Mateo Sagasta, one of those mobile politicians who always fall on their feet whatever happens, and Francisco Silvela, who may be described as a Liberal-Conservative in contrast to Cánovas, who was a Tory of the old school, and aspired to be a despot. Toryism, though the word is unknown there, dies hard in Spain; but there are not wanting signs that the Conservatives of the new school have the progress and emancipation of the country quite as much at heart as any Liberal. It was the Conservative *Nacional* that in a leading article of March 29th in 1901, under the head of " Vicious Customs," called attention to the crowds of place-hunters who invade the public offices after a change of ministry, and to the barefaced impudence of some of their claims for preferment. " The remedy is in the hands of the advisers of the Crown," it continued. " Let them shut the doors of their offices against influence and intrigue, keep *Empleados* of acknowledged competence permanently in their posts, and not appoint new ones without the conviction that they have capacity and aptitude for the work they will have to do. By this means, if the problem be not entirely solved, it will at least be in train for a solution satisfactory at once for a good administration and for the highest interests of the State."

The way in which the wire-pulling is done from Madrid, in case of an election, is through the *cacique*, or chief person in each constituency; hence the name of the process. This person may be the Civil Governor, the *Alcalde*, or merely a rich landowner or large employer of labour in touch with the Government: the pressure brought to bear may be of two sorts, taking the form of bribery or threat. The voters who hang on to the skirts of the *cacique* may hope for Government employment, or they may fear a sudden call to pay up arrears of rent or of taxes; the hint is given from headquarters, or a Government candidate is sent down. It matters little how the thing is done so long as the desired end is accomplished. Speaking of the general election which took place last June, and in which it was well known beforehand that the Liberals were to be returned in a large majority, one of the Madrid newspapers wrote: " The people will vote, but assuredly the deputies sent up to the Cortes will not be *their* representatives, nor their choice."

We, who have for so many years enjoyed a settled government, forget how different all this is in a country like Spain, which has oftener had to be reproached for enduring bad government than for a readiness to effect violent changes, or to try new experiments; but the progress actually made since the Revolution of 1868 has really been extraordinary, and it has gone steadily forward. Spain has always been celebrated for the making of *convenios*—a word which is scarcely correctly translated by " arrangement." During the Carlist wars, the Government, and even generals in command, made *convenios* with the insurgents to allow convoys to pass without interference, money value sometimes being a factor in the case; but one of the strangest of these out-of-sight agree-

ments, and one which English people never
understand, is that which has existed almost ever
since the Restoration between the political parties
in the Congress, or, at least, between their leaders. It is an arrangement, loyally carried out,
by which each party is allowed in turn to come
into power. The Cortes is elected to suit the
party whose turn it is to be in office, and there is
little reality in the apparent differences. Silvela
and Sagasta go backwards and forwards with the
regularity of a pendulum, and the country goes on
its way improving its position daily and hourly,
with small thanks to its Government.

Perhaps it is as well! It gives assurance, at
least, that no particularly wild schemes or subversive changes shall be made. When one administration has almost wrecked the ship, as in
the Caserta marriage, the other comes in peace-
fully, and sets the public mind at rest; both parties
wish for peace and quietness, and no more revolutions, and the political seesaw keeps the helm fairly
straight in ordinary weather. To what extent
the insane and disastrous policy which led to the
war with America by its shilly-shally treatment
of Cuba, now promising autonomy, now putting
down the grinding heel of tyranny, and to what
extent the suicidal action of the oscillating parties
—for both share the responsibility—in their in-
structions to their generals and admirals, and the
astounding unpreparedness for war of any kind,
still less with a country like America, may be

traced to this system of "arrangements," which allows one party to hand its responsibilities over to the other, one can only guess. It is to be hoped that when the two figureheads at present before the country go over to the majority, there may come to the front some earnest and truly patriotic ministers, who have been quietly training in the school of practical politics, and can take the helm with some hope of doing away with the crying evils of *empleomania* and *caciquismo*. Until then there will be no political greatness for Spain.

The advance which Spain has made, " in spite of her Governments, and not by their assistance," has been remarkable in past years. Since the beginning of the last century she has gone through a series of political upheavals and disasters which might well have destroyed any country; and, in fact, her division into so many differing nationalities has, perhaps, been her greatest safeguard. Even after the Revolution of 1868 the series of events through which she passed was enough to have paralysed her whole material prosperity; the actual loss in materials, and still more in the lives of her sons, during the fratricidal wars at home and in her colonies, is incalculable, and that she was not ruined, but, on the contrary, advanced steadily in industry and commerce during the whole time, shows her enormous inherent vitality. Since then she has undergone the lamentable war with America, has lost her chief colonies, and the Peninsula has been well-nigh swamped by the *repatriados* from Cuba, returning to their native country penniless and, in many cases, worn out.   And yet the state of Spain was never so promising, her steady progress never more assured.   Looking back to the Revolution, it will be enough to name some of the measures secured for the benefit of the people.   They include complete civil and religious liberty, with reforms in the administration of the laws and the condition of prisoners, liberty of education, and the spread of normal schools into every corner of the Peninsula, the establishment of savings banks for the poor, somewhat on the lines of England's Post Office Savings Bank; railways have received an enormous impulse; quays and breakwaters have been erected, so that every portion of the kingdom is now in immediate touch with Madrid; while the universities are sending forth daily young men thoroughly trained as engineers, electricians, doctors, and scientists of every variety to take the places which some years ago were almost necessarily filled by foreigners for want of trained native talent.

Local government in the smaller towns of the Peninsula is generally said to be very good, and to work with great smoothness and efficiency hand-in-hand with centralised authority in Madrid.   The fusion of the varying nationalities is gradually gaining ground, and the hard-and-fast line between the provinces is disappearing.

There is more nationality now in matters of everyday life than there has ever been before. In old times it needed the touch of a foreign hand, the threat of foreign interference, to rouse the nation as one man. Commerce and industry and the national emulation between province and province are doing gradually what it once needed the avarice of a Napoleon to evoke.

The paper constitutions of Spain have been many, beginning with that of 1812, which the Liberals tried to force on Ferdinand VII., to that of 1845, which the Conservatives look upon as the ideal, or that of 1869, embodying all that the Revolution had gained from absolutism, including manhood suffrage. In the first Cortes summoned after the Restoration, thanks to the good sense of Castelar, the Republican party, from being conspirators, became a parliamentary party in opposition. Zorilla alone, looking upon it as a sham, retired to France in disgust. By the new constitution of 1876, the power of making laws remained, as before, vested in the Cortes and the Crown: the Senate consists of three classes, Grandes, Bishops, and high officers of State sitting by right, with one hundred members nominated by the Crown, and one hundred and eighty elected by provincial Councils, universities, and other corporations. Half of the elected members go out every five years. The deputies to the Congress are elected by indirect vote on a residential manhood suffrage, and they number four

hundred and thirty-one. A certain number of
equal electoral districts of fifty thousand inhabitants elect one member each; and twenty-six large
districts, having several representatives, send
eighty-eight members to the Cortes. Every province has its provincial elective Council, managing
its local affairs, and each commune its separate
District Council, with control over local taxation.
Yet, though ostensibly free, these local bodies are
practically in the power of the political wire-
puller, or *cacique*.

CHAPTER X

COMMERCE AND AGRICULTURE

COMMERCE and industry had progressed by leaps and bounds even during the disastrous and troublous years between the expulsion of Isabel II. and the restoration of her son. The progress is now much more steady and more diffused over the whole country, but it is by no means less remarkable, especially taking into consideration the disaster of the war with America and the loss to Spain of her old colonies.

Among her politicians in past times there were never wanting those who considered that the loss of Cuba would be a distinct gain to the mother country, and perhaps it may be safely said that since the colony had not only been for so many years the forcing-house of bureaucratic corruption, but had also drained the resources of Spain both of money and lives to the extreme limit of her possibility, she is more likely now to regain her old position among European nations, when left at peace to develop her enormous resources and set her house in order without the distraction of war, either at home or abroad.

When one remembers that this happy condition has never obtained in the country since the death of Ferdinand VII. until the close of the Spanish-American War, and that the country is only now recovering from the disorganisation caused by the return of her troops and refugees from Cuba and Manila, it is not surprising to find that the activity manifested in her trade, her manufactures, and her industries is such as to give the greatest hopes for her future to her own people and to those who watch her from afar with friendly eyes.

Whichever we may regard as cause or effect, the progress of the country has been very largely identified with the extension of her railway system. It must have been a great step towards liberal education when the country which, priding herself on her geographical position and her rich internal resources, had hitherto wrapped herself in her national *capa*, and considered that she was amply sufficient to herself, condescended to throw open her mountain barriers to immigrants. It was not until 1848 that the first Spanish railway was opened, and it was but seventeen miles in length; but in the next ten years five hundred miles had been constructed, and between 1858 and 1868 no fewer than two thousand eight hundred and five miles, the Pyrenees had been pierced, and direct communication with the rest of Europe accomplished.

During the troublous years following the Revolution and the melancholy struggles of the second

Carlist war, very little progress was made. Foreign capital, which had hitherto been invested in
Spanish railways, was naturally frightened away,
and the Northern Railway itself, the great artery
to France, was constantly being torn up and dam-
aged, and the lives of the passengers endangered,
by the armed mobs which infested the country,
and were supposed by some people to represent
the cause of legitimacy, and which had, in fact,
the sanction of the Church and of the Pope. It
was not, in the majority of cases, that the people
sympathised with Don Carlos, but it was easier
and more amusing for the lazy and the ne'er-
do-weels to receive pay and rations for carrying a gun, and taking pot-shots at any object
that presented itself, human or other, than to
work in the fields, the mines, or on the railways. Hence public enterprise was paralysed;
again and again the workmen, with no desire of
their own, were driven off by superior bands of
these wandering shooters, who scarcely deserved
even the name of guerillas, and public works
were left deserted and decaying, while the commerce and industry of the province were wrecked,
and apparently destroyed irrevocably.

In the earlier stages of railway construction
and management, French capital and French
labour were employed. England held aloof,
partly on account of the closing of the London
Stock Exchange to Spanish enterprises, in consequence of the vexed question of the celebrated

coupons, but also because the aid afforded by the State did not fall in with the ideas of English capitalists. They desired a guaranteed rate of interest, while the Spanish Government would have nothing but a subvention paid down in one lump sum, arguing that it would be impossible to tell when a line was making more than the guaranteed interest, "as the companies would so arrange their accounts as to show invariably an interest smaller than that guaranteed!" With this view of the honesty of their own officials, no one else could be expected to have a better opinion of them; and England allowed France and Belgium thenceforward to find all the capital and all the materials for Spanish railways.

The total amount of subventions actually paid by Government up to December 31, 1882, was £24,529,148. "If," says the author of *Commercial and Industrial Spain*, "the money that we so candidly lent to the swarm of defaulting South American Republics had been properly invested in Spanish railways, a great deal of trouble might probably have been spared to the unfortunate investors."

All that, however, is altered now: the State schools and universities are turning out daily well-equipped native engineers, both for railway and mining works, and Spaniards are finding their own capital for public works. The phrase "Spain for the Spaniards" is acquiring a new significance—perhaps the most hopeful of all the signs of progress the country is making. In 1899, there were working 12,916 kilómetros of railways, or 7.9 kilómetros for each 10,000 of the population. A kilómetro equals 1.609 English mile. There is no part of the country now isolated, either from the centre of government in Madrid, or from the coast, and communication with Portugal, and, through France, with the rest of Europe, is easy and constant. With this advance in means of transit, the trade of the country has received an immense impulse, and its raw and manufactured goods are now reaching all markets.

The rich mineral wealth of the country and its wonderful climate only need enlightened enterprise to make Spain one of the richest and most important commercial factors in the world's trade. The list of minerals alone, raised from mines in working, amounts to twenty-two, ranging from gold and silver, copper, tin, zinc, quick-silver, salt, coal, etc., to cobalt and antimony; and 8,313,-218 tons of minerals of all these twenty-two classes were raised in 1882 against 1,201,054 in 1862. The value of mines in 1880 was represented by one hundred and eleven millions of pesetas (francs), but in 1898 by three hundred and nineteen millions (pesetas). The value of imports in 1882 was 816,666,901 pesetas, and of exports 765,376,-087 pesetas. In 1899, imports were 1,045,391,983, and exports 864,367,885. But this is taking exactly the period covered by the war with America; a fairer estimate of exports is that of

1897, which stood at 1,074,883,372. No statement has been published since 1899, but inter-
mediate statistics show the trade of the country
to be advancing rapidly.

To return, however, to Spanish industries.
In late years large smelting-works have been
opened in Spain, with Spanish capital and management, while at Bilbao are large iron-works for
the manufacture of steel rails. There are splendid deposits of iron in the country, and as the
duty on foreign rails entering Spain is £3 4s. per
ton, it is probable that the near future will see
the country free from the necessity of importing
manufactured iron, or, in fact, metal of any kind.
A Catalan company has established important
works for reducing the sulphur of the rich mines
near Lorca, and confidently expects to produce
some thirty thousand tons of sulphur per annum.
The rich silver mines of the Sierra Almagrera are
almost wholly in native hands, and have already
yielded large fortunes to the owners. With the
present improved transport and shipping facilities
in every part of the country, it is probable that
the valuable mines scattered all over the Peninsula will be thoroughly worked, to the advance
of commercial and industrial interests over the
entire country.

While the seaboard provinces are rich in fish-
eries, as well as in mines, in the south the country
is able to grow rice, sugar-cane, maize, raisins,
as well as wheat, olives, oranges, grapes, dates,

11

bananas, pine-apples, and almost all kinds of tropical fruits. The cultivation of all varieties of fruit and vegetables, and their careful gathering and packing have become the object of many large companies and private individuals. Dates, bananas, grapes, plums, tomatoes, melons, as well as asparagus and other early vegetables, are now being shipped to foreign markets as regular articles of trade, in a condition which insures a rapid and increasing sale. The exportation of fruit has doubled within the last few years. The production of cane sugar in 1899 was thirty-one thousand tons, or exactly three times the amount of that produced in 1889. The exportation of wine, which in 1894 was two millions of milelitros, was in 1898 nearly five millions, and it is daily increasing (one gallon English measure equals about four and one half litros).

Spain has always had excellent wines unknown to other countries, besides that which is manufactured into what we know as "sherry"; but many of them were so carelessly made as to be unfit for transit abroad. The attention of wine-growers has, however, been steadily turned to this subject during the last twenty years; greater care has been taken in the production; the best methods have been ascertained and followed, and it is possible now to obtain undoctored Spanish wines which perfectly bear the carriage in cask without injury; and, to meet a direct sale to the customer, small barrels containing about twelve gallons are shipped from Tarragona and other ports to England.

One of the most hopeful signs of the economic awakening of the country is the establishment of the *Boletin de la Cámara de Comercio de España en la Gran Bretáña*, published each month in London.

In this little commercial circular a review is given of the commerce and industry of all nations during the month; all fluctuations are noted, extracts from foreign statistics or money articles given, suggestions made for the opening up of Spanish commerce, and the introduction of her manufactures into this and other countries. Speaking on the question of the introduction of pure Spanish wines into England, a recent writer in the *Boletin* remarks that English workmen are thirsty animals, that they like a big drink, but they are not really desirous of becoming intoxicated by it. In fact, they would most of them prefer to be able to drink more without bad effects. The writer goes on to say that if the English workman could obtain pure wine that would cost no more than his customary beer, and would not make him intoxicated, and if Spanish light wines —which he says could be sold in England for less than good beer—were offered in tempting-looking taverns and under pleasant conditions, he believes that a really enormous trade would be the result, to the benefit of both nations. The suggestion is, at least, an interesting one, and though the scheme would certainly not benefit the habitual

drunkard, who becomes enamoured of his own
debauchery, it might be very welcome to many
of the working people, who, as " our neighbour "
quaintly remarks, like a big drink, but do not
necessarily wish to become intoxicated.

In this connection, it may be interesting to know
that the small twelve-gallon casks of red wine, resembling Burgundy rather than claret, but less
heavy than the Australian wines, and forming a
delicious drink with water, are delivered at one's
own door carriage free for a price which works
out, including duty, at $8\frac{1}{2}d$. the ordinary bottle,
or 1s. 2d. the flagon, such as the Australian wine
is sold in. This is, in fact, cheaper than good
stout or ale.

Spain has always been celebrated for two special
manufactures—her silk and woollen goods; but
for very many years these have been almost unknown beyond her own boundaries. In the time
of the Moors her silken goods had a world-wide
fame; and the silk-worm has been cultivated there
probably from the earliest days, when it was sur-
reptitiously introduced into Europe. Groves of
mulberry trees were grown especially for sericul-
ture in the irrigated provinces of the South, the
care of the insect being undertaken by the women, while the men were employed on tasks more
suitable to their strength. Native-grown spun
and woven silk forms such an important part in
the national costumes of the people that it has
attained to great perfection without attracting

much foreign notice. The silk petticoats of the women, the velvet jackets and trunk hose of the men, the beautiful silk and woollen *mantas*, with their deep fringes of silken or woollen balls; the *madroños*, or silk tufts and balls, used as decorations for the Andalusian or the gypsy hats, not to mention the beautifully soft and pure silks of Barcelona, or the silk laces made in such perfection in many parts of the country,—all these are objects of merchandise only needing to be known, to occasion a large demand, especially in these days when the French invention of weighted dyes floods the English market with something that has the outward appearance of silk, but which does not even wait for wear to disclose its real nature, but rots into holes on the drapers' shelves, and would-be smart young women of slender purses walk about in what has been well called "tin attire," in the manufacture of which the silk-worm has had only the slenderest interest.

The blankets and rugs of Palencia have been known to some few English people for many years, owing to their extreme lightness, great warmth, and literally unending wear; but it is only within the last very few years that they can be said to have had any market at all in England, and now they are called "Pyrenean" rather than Spanish goods. One of the suggestions of the little commercial circular already referred to is that Spaniards should open depots or special agencies all over England for the sale of their woollen goods, after the manner of the Jaeger Company.

The flocks of merino sheep to be seen on the wooded slopes of the Pyrenees, and all over Estremadura, following their shepherd after the manner with which Old Testament history makes us familiar, are said to be direct descendants of the old Arabian flocks, and certainly the appearance of one of these impassive-looking shepherds leading his flock to " green pastures, and beside the still waters," takes one back in the world's history in a way that few other things do. The flock know the voice of their shepherd, and follow him unquestioningly wheresoever he goes; there is no driving, no hurrying; and the same may be said of the pigs, which form such an important item in the social economy of a Spanish peasant's home.

Staying once at Castellon de la Plana, in Valencia, my delight was to watch the pig-herd and his troop. Early in the morning, at a fixed hour, he issued from his house in one of the small alleys, staff in hand, and with a curious kind of horn or whistle. This he blew as he walked along, from time to time, without turning his head, in that strange trance of passivity which distinguishes the Valencian peasant. Out from dark corners, narrow passages, mud hovels on all sides, came tearing along little pigs, big pigs, dark, light, fat, thin pigs,—pigs of every description,—and joined the procession headed by this sombre-looking herdsman, with his long stick and his blue-and-white striped *manta* thrown over his shoulder. By the time he had reached the end of the village he had a large herd following him. Then the whole party slowly disappeared in the distance, under the groves of cork-trees or up the mountain paths. The evening performance was more amusing still. Just about sundown the stately herdsman again appeared with his motley following. He took no manner of notice of them. He stalked majestically towards his own particular hovel, and at each corner of a lane or group of cottages the pigs said " Good night " to each other by a kick-up of their heels and a whisk of their curly little tails, and scampered off home by themselves, until, at the end of the village, only one solitary pig was following his leader — probably they shared one home between them. It seemed a peaceful, if not an absolutely happy, life!

One would expect a country with such a climate, or rather with so many climates, as Spain, to make a great feature of agriculture. It can at once produce wheat of the very finest quality, wine, oil, rice, sugar, and every kind of fruit and vegetable that is known; and it ought to be able to support a large agricultural population in comfort, and export largely. Taking into account, also, the rich mineral wealth, which should make her independent of imports of this nature, it is sad to see that in past years, even so late as 1882, wheat and flour, coal and coke, iron and tools figure amongst her imports—the first two in very large proportions. Although the vast plains of Estremadura and Castile produce the finest wheat known to commerce, the quantity, owing to the want of water, is so small in relation to the acreage under cultivation, that it does not suffice for home consumption, except in very favourable years; while the utilisation of the magnificent rivers, which now roll their waters uselessly to the sea, would make the land what it once was when the thrifty Moor held it—a thickly populated and flourishing grain-producing district. In place of the wandering flocks of sheep and pigs gaining a precarious existence on the herbage left alive by the blistering sun on an arid soil, there should be smiling homesteads and blooming gardens everywhere, trees and grateful shade where now the ground, between the rainy seasons, becomes all of one dusty, half-burnt colour, reminding one more of the " back of a mangy camel," as it has been described, than of a country that has once been fruitful and productive.

The late General Concha, Marqués del Duero, was the originator of sugar-cane cultivation. He spent a large portion of his private fortune in establishing what bids fair to be one of the most productive industries of his country. But, like most pioneers of progress, he reaped no benefit himself. His fine estates near Malaga, with their productive cane-farms, passed into other hands before he had reaped the reward of his patriotic endeavours. For a long time the cheap, bounty-fed beet sugars of Germany, which never approach beyond being an imitation of real sugar—as every housewife can testify who has tried to make jam with them—were able to undersell the produce of the cane; but the latest statistics show that this industry is now making steady progress, the production of 1899 being thirty-one thousand tons, or exactly three times that of 1899. *À propos* of the difference between cane and beet sugars for all domestic purposes, and the superior cheapness of the more costly article, it is satisfactory to note that in England the working classes, through their own co-operative societies, insist on being supplied with the former, knowing by experimental proof its immense superiority; and one may hope that their wisdom may spread into households where the servants pull the wires, and care nothing about economy.

Looking at the ordinary map of Spain, it appears to be ridiculous to say that the greater part of the country is in want of water. Although it is intersected by three large ranges of mountains beyond the Pyrenees, and innumerable others of smaller dimensions, thus making a great proportion of the country impossible for agriculture, it is rich in magnificent rivers and in smaller ones, all of which are allowed to run to waste in many parts of the country, while even a small portion of their waters, artificially dammed and utilised for irrigation, if only of the lands lying on each side of them, would mean wealth and prosperity and an abounding population where now the "everlasting sun" pours its rays over barren wastes. Moreover, by the growth of the wood, which once covered the plains and has been cut down, little by little, until the whole surface of the land was changed, in process of time the climate would become less dry, and vegetation more rapid and easy.

Ever since the expulsion of the Moors from Castile and Estremadura, the land has been allowed gradually to go almost out of cultivation for want of water, the wholesale devastation of forests, in combination with the lapse of all irrigation, acting as a constantly accelerating cause for the arid and unproductive condition of the once genial soil. Irrigation has been the crying want of Spain for generations past; but even now the Government scarcely seems to have awakened to its necessity. Perhaps, however, the Spaniard who goes on his way, never troubling to listen to the opinion or advice of his neighbour, has not, after all, been so wanting in common sense as some of the more energetic of his critics have thought. In spite of all the changes and disasters of successive Governments, a steady and rapid advance has been made in providing means of transport and shipping, by the construction of railways to every part of the country, the making and keeping in condition of admirable highways, and the building of breakwaters and quays in many of the seaports, so that now the output of the mines and produce of all kinds can find market within the country, or be shipped abroad freely.

If the money no longer being expended in railways and docks were now devoted to irrigation wherever it is needed, a rapid change would become apparent over the whole face of the country, and the population would increase in proportion as the land would bear it. Irrigation works have been more than once undertaken by the aid of foreign money, and under the charge of foreign engineers; but the people themselves—the landowners and peasant proprietors—were not ripe for it, and, alas! some of the canals which would have turned whole valleys into gardens have been allowed to go to ruin, or to become actually obliterated, while the scanty crops are raised once in two or three years from the same soil, which will yield three crops in one year by the help of water. Difficulties arose about the sale of the water—a prolific cause of dispute even in the old irrigated districts—and the people said: " What do we want with water, except what comes from heaven ? If the Virgin thinks we want water, she sends it." Fitting result of the teaching of the Church for so many years, with the example ever held up for admiration of the patron saint, Isidro, who knelt all day at his prayers, and left the tilling of his fields to the angels! It would seem that these ministers of grace are not good husbandmen, since the land became the arid waste it now is, while successive Isidros have been engaged in religious duties, which they were taught were all that was necessary.

As an example of what irrigation means in the sunlit fields of Spain, an acre of irrigable land in Valencia or Murcia sells for prices varying from £150 to £400, according to its quality or its situation, while land not irrigable only fetches sums varying from £7 to £20. In Castile, land would not in any case fetch so high a price as that which has been under irrigated cultivation for centuries past; but in any district the value of dry land is never more than a twelfth of what it is when irrigable. In truth, however, there is more than irrigation needed to bring the lands of Castile and Estremadura into profitable cultivation, and it cannot be done without the expenditure of large sums of money at the outset in manures, and good implements in place of the obsolete old implements with which the ground is now scratched rather than ploughed. Given good capital and intelligent farming, as in the irrigated districts, and two, and even three, crops a year can be raised in unceasing succession; lucern gives from ten to twelve cuttings in one year, fifteen days being sufficient for the growth of a new crop.

I have pointed out what one day's sun can do in raising grass seed in Madrid, which stands on the highest point of the elevated table-land occupying the centre of Spain. Seeing that the principal item of the revenue is derived from the land tax, and that it is calculated on the value of the land, it would appear to be the first interest of an enlightened government to foster irrigation in every possible way, and encourage agriculture and the planting of trees.

Although the people of Spain have hated their more immediate neighbours with an exceeding bitter hatred,—as, indeed, they had good cause to do in the past,—her public men have had a strange fancy for importing or imitating French customs. One that militates more than anything else against agricultural prosperity is the law of inheritance, copied from the French. By this the State divides an estate amongst the heirs without any reference to the wishes of the proprietor at his death. Not only are all large estates broken up and practically dissipated, so that it is to no one's interest to improve his property or spend money on it, but the small farms of the peasant proprietor are broken into smaller fragments in the same way; and it is no uncommon thing to see a field of a few acres divided into six or eight furrows, none of them enough to support one man. While he has to go off seeking work where he can get it, his strip of land clings to him like a curse, for he must lose his work if he would try to cultivate it, and at his death it will again be subdivided, until at last there is nothing left to share. Meanwhile, the land, which is not enough to be of any value to anyone, has been allowed to go almost out of cultivation; or if it bear anything at all, it is weeds.

Until some remedy be found for this enervating system, it would seem as if Spanish agriculture is doomed to remain in its present unsatisfactory condition over a great part of the kingdom. The improvement of agriculture is practically a question of private enterprise, and under the existing law of inheritance neither enterprise nor interest can be expected of the small proprietor; nor indeed of the large landowner, who knows that, whatever he may do to improve his estate, it is doomed to be cut to pieces and divided amongst his next of kin until it is eventually extinguished. Whether, in some future time, an enlightened scheme of co-operation could work the arid lands into cultivation again, if the Government would give the necessary aid in the form of irrigation, remains among the unanswered riddles of the future. Prophecy in Spain is never possible; it is always the unexpected which happens in that country of sharp contradictions. All one can do is to note past progress and the drift of the present current, which, whatever government is at the nominal head of affairs, seems to be towards widespread—in fact, quite general—advance both in knowledge and industrial activity.

The greatest hope for the future lies in the fact that it is no longer foreign money or foreign labour that is working for the good of the country; the impulse is from within, and every penny of capital that is sunk in public works, manufactures, or industrial enterprise, is so much invested in a settled state of affairs. When the individual has everything to lose by revolutionary changes, when the commerce of the country is becoming too important to be allowed to be upset easily, and it is everybody's interest to support and increase it, the main body of the people are ranged on the side of peace and progress. They have had enough of civil war, enough of tyranny; they have achieved freedom, and want nothing so much as to taste of it in quietness.

To revert for a moment to the special manufactures of the country, it appears to be the wise policy of the powers that be in Spain to-day to encourage, by every possible means, native industries and the development of the rich resources of the country. If it be only in the superior education required of the workmen, and the drawing out of their natural talents, the movement is an immense gain to the people, so long purposely kept in a condition of slothful ignorance.

Besides the woollen manufactures of Palencia, Lorca, Jerez, Barcelona, Valencia, and other places, are many cloth factories in Cataluña, as well as others for the production of silk fabrics, lace, and very high-class embroideries, for which last Spain has long been famous, but which have hitherto been little known beyond her own frontiers. In artistic crafts may be named the pottery works of Pickman, Mesaque, Gomez, and others in Seville, where magnificent reproductions of Moorish and Hespaño-Moresque tiles and pottery are being turned out; there are also factories for this class of goods in Valencia, Barcelona, Segovia, Talevera, and many other places. Ornamental iron and damascene work holds the high reputation which Spain has never lost, but the output is very largely increased. Gold and silver inlaid on iron, iron inlaid on copper and silver, are some of the forms of this beautiful work. That executed in Madrid differs from that of Toledo, Eibar, and other centres of the craft. The iron gate-work executed in Madrid and Barcelona is very hard to beat, and the casting of bronzes is carried out with every modern improvement. The wood-carvers of Spain have always been famous, and the craft appears to be in no danger of falling behind its old reputation, much beautiful decorative work of this description being produced for modern needs. The *Circulo de Artes* holds an exhibition in Madrid every other year, and in the intervening years the Government has one, in the large permanent buildings erected for the purpose at the end of the Fuente Castellana. The manufacture of artistic furniture and other connected industries are encouraged also by a bi-yearly exhibition in Madrid, where prizes and commendations are given. The chief centres of artistic furniture-making are Madrid, Barcelona, Granada, and Zaragoza. Exhibitions of arts and

crafts and of all kinds of industries and manufactures are also held, at intervals, in the principal
towns all over the country.   An interesting exhibition of Spanish and South American produc-
tions was held in 1901 in Bilbao with great success.

Nor ought we to forget the industry for which
Seville is famed.   The manufacture of tobacco
is almost wholly in the hands of women, and is
a very important industry, thousands being employed in the large factories making up cigars,
cigarettes, and preparing and packing the finer
kinds of tobacco.   The cigar-girl of Seville is a
well-known type, almost as much dreaded by the
authorities as admired by her own class.   The
women are mostly young, and often attractive,
extremely pronounced both in dress and manners,
and are quite a power to be reckoned with when
they choose to assert themselves.   On more than
one occasion they have taken up some cause *en
masse*, and have gathered in thousands, determined to have their way.

When this happens, the powers that be are
reduced to great straits.   Neither the *Guardia
Civile* nor the military can be relied on to use
force, and unless the army of irate women can be
persuaded to retire from the contest it is probable
that, relying with perfect confidence on the privileges of their sex, they will gain what they consider their rights—at all events their will.

No country in the world is more suited for
manufactures and exports than Spain.   She has

an unexampled seaboard, and many magnificent natural harbours, and now an easy approach through Portugal to the sea, even if her own ports should be insufficient. Common commercial interests are likely to bring that Iberian kingdom or commonwealth to pass which has been the dream of some of her politicians, and is still cherished in parts of both countries. The northern ports in the Atlantic are, perhaps, the most important; that of Bilbao, a most unpromising one by nature, has grown out of all recognition since the close of the Carlist war. The railway to the iron mines was already in course of construction when the war broke out; everything was stopped, the workmen carried off willy-nilly to join the marauding bands of the Pretender, the town—which boasts that it has never been taken, although twice almost demolished during the two insane civil wars—was wrecked and well-nigh ruined, its industries destroyed, its commerce at an end. With peace and quietness came one of the most extraordinary revivals of modern times: the population increased at a marvellous rate, the new town sprang into existence on the left bank of the Nerrion, the river was deepened, the bar, which used to block almost all entrance, practically removed, extensive dock-works carried out; so that in ten years the shipment of ore from the port sprang up from four hundred and twenty-five thousand tons to 3,737,176, and is increasing daily. Bilbao, with its five railway stations, its electric tramways, and its population of sixty-six thousand, has become the first and most important shipping outlet of Spain. Nor have the southern ports of Huelva and Seville been much behind it in their rapid progress; while on the Mediterranean coast are Malaga, Almería, Aguilas, Cartagena, Valencia, and Tarragona—all vying with the older, and once singular, centre of commercial and industrial activity, Barcelona. The northwest seaboard has been hitherto somewhat behind the movement, owing to a less complete railway communication with the rest of the country; now that this is no more a reproach, the fine natural harbours of Rivadeo, Vivero, Carril, Pontevedra, Vigo, and Coruña, are gradually following suit, some with more vigour than others. The little land-locked harbour of Pasages has for some years been rapidly rising to the rank of a first-class shipping port.

It is satisfactory to note, from the latest statistics, that in 1899 Spain possessed a total of one thousand and thirty-five merchant ships, that in the same year she bought from England alone sixty-seven, and that 17,419 ships, carrying 11,-857,674 tons of exports, left Spanish ports for foreign markets. Although no official information has been published since that year, the increase since the close of the war has been in very much greater ratio. From the same records we find that during the year 1899 no fewer than sixty-nine large companies were formed, of which twenty-three were for shipping, eight were new sugar factories, seven banks, seven mining, six electric, and ten others related either to manufacture or commerce, the total capital of these new enterprises representing one hundred and twenty-eight millions of pesetas.

In contrast to Portugal, the *caminos reales*, or high-roads, of Spain have long been very good. It is true that where these State roads do not exist, the unadulterated *arroyo* serves as a country road, or a mere track across the fields made by carts and foot-passengers, and when an obstruction occurs in the form of too deep a hole to be got through, the track takes a turn outside it, and returns to the direct line as soon as circumstances permit. An *arroyo* is given in the dictionary as "a rivulet"; it is, in fact, generally a rushing torrent during the rains, eating its way through the land, and laying down a smooth, deep layer of sand, or even soil, between high banks. Immediately after the rainy season this affords a firm, good road for a time, but eventually it becomes ploughed into impassable ruts by the wheels of the carts, unless trampled hard by the feet of passing flocks.

Government undertakes the cost and the superintendence of the *caminos reales*, and does it well. The corps of engineers is modelled on French lines, and is a department of the Ministry of Public Works. The course of study is extremely severe, and the examinations are strict and searching. When a candidate passes, he is appointed assistant-engineer by the Ministry, and he rises in his profession solely by seniority. Every province has its engineer-in-chief, with his staff of assistants; the superintendents of harbours, railways, and other public works are specially appointed from qualified engineers. In addition to the care of the construction and repair of all highways and Government works in his district, the engineer-in-chief has the overlooking of all works which, although they may be the result of private enterprise and private capital, are authorised or carried out under Government concession. These concessions are only granted after the project has been submitted to, and approved by, the Ministry of Public Works, and it passes under the supervision of the engineer of the provinces. In old days, if not now, there was a good deal of " the itching palm " about the officials, not excluding the Minister himself, through whose hands the granting of concessions passed, even the wives coming in for handsome presents and " considerations," without which events had a knack of not moving; and when the army of *Empleados* became *Cesantes*, this work, of course, began all over again. The railway engineers form a separate body, the country being mapped out into arbitrary divisions, each under the charge of one engineer-in-chief, with a large body of assistants.

The telegraph system of Spain has now for many years been in a good condition. The construction of the lines dates from about 1862, when only five miles were in operation. There is now probably not a village in the whole country that does not possess its telegraph office, and in all the important towns this is kept open all night. A peseta for twenty words, including the address, is the uniform charge, every additional word being ten centimos. The telegraphs were established by the Government, and are under its control. All railway lines of public service, and those which receive a subvention, must provide two wires for Government use. Telephones are now in use in all large centres, and electric lighting and traction are far more widely used than in England.

CHAPTER XI

THE ARMY AND NAVY

IT is not necessary to say to anyone who has the smallest acquaintance with history that Spaniards are naturally brave and patriotic. The early history of the Peninsula is one of valour in battle, whether by land or sea. The standard of Castile has been borne by her sons triumphantly over the surface of the globe. Few of us now remember that Johnson wrote of the Spain of his day:

> Has Heaven reserved, in pity to the poor,
> No pathless waste, no undiscovered shore,
> No secret island on the trackless main,
> No peaceful desert, yet unclaimed by Spain?

In the old days when Drake undertook to " singe the King of Spain's beard," and carried out his threat, our sailors and those of Philip II., some time " King of England," as the Spaniards still insist on calling him, met often in mortal combat, and learned to recognise and honour in each other the same dogged fighting-power, the same discipline and quiet courage. The picture of the Spaniards standing bareheaded in token of reverence and admiration of a worthy foe, as some small English ships went down with all their crew rather than surrender, in those old days of strife, touches a chord which still vibrates in memory of battles fought and won together by Englishmen and Spaniards under the Iron Duke. True, some battered and torn English flags hang as trophies in the armoury of Madrid, but one likes to remember that in the only battle where our colours were lost, the Spanish troops were commanded by an Englishman, James Stuart, Duke of Berwick, the direct ancestor of the present Duque de Berwick y Alva, and the English by one of French birth. In every case where foreign foes have invaded Spain, sooner or later they have been driven out. *Santiago! y Cierra España!* was the war-cry which roused every child of Spain to close his beloved country to alien domination.

Unfortunately, the yoke of the foreigner came in more invidious guise. From the death of Ferdinand and Isabella to the year 1800, the sons of Spain were immolated to serve causes which were of no account to her, to protect the interests of sovereigns who had nothing in common with her provinces, to add to the power of the Austrian Hapsburgs and the French Bourbons. We have seen how the people whom Napoleon had believed to be sunk in fanaticism, dead to all national aspiration, the mere slaves of a despicable King, and the sport of his debauched Queen and her lover, sprang to arms and drove the invader from their land. So would it be to-day if the country were even threatened by foreign invasion. " The dogs of Spain," as Granville called them, know well how to protect their soil.

Within comparatively recent years the campaign in Morocco, and the expeditionary force sent to Cochin-China, showed that the Spanish army was not to be despised. It has been the misfortune of Spain that her soldiers have too often had the melancholy task of fighting against their own people, or those of their colonies, both of whom have been excited and aided in insurrection for years by foreign contributions of arms and money. In these unhappy fratricidal struggles the fighting has never been more than half-hearted, and during the numerous military *pronunciamientos* it has often been necessary to keep the troops from meeting, as they could never be trusted not to fraternise; and after the first abortive attempt by Prim to effect the revolution which later freed the country, the curious spectacle was afforded of Prim and his soldiers marching quietly out of one end of a village, while the troops of the Queen, sent in pursuit, were being purposely kept back from marching too quickly in at the other.

The army of Spain would seem to suffer from a plethora of officers, especially those of the highest rank. In the time of Alfonso XII., there were ten marshals, fifty-five generals, sixty-six *maris-cales de campo*, and one hundred and ninety-seven brigadiers; adding those on the retired list liable for service, there were in all five hundred and twenty generals, four hundred and seventy-two colonels, eight hundred and ninety-four lieuten-ant-colonels, 2113 commandants, 5041 captains, 5880 lieutenants, and 4833 sous-lieutenants. With such an array of officers, it is scarcely to be won-dered at that promotion in the ordinary way was looked on as impossible, and the juggle of military *pronunciamientos* was regarded as almost the only means of rising in the army. It was no uncom-mon thing to promise a rise of one grade through-out a whole corps to compass one of these miniature revolutions. However, all that is happily past. General Weyler, — whose name indicates alien blood at some period of his family history, —the present Minister of War, has taken the thorough reform of the army in hand, though it is too soon to say if he will be as successful as is generally expected from his known energy and common sense, since the work is only now in progress.

One of the most fertile sources of disturbance in the old days of Isabel II. was the presence of the *primo sargentos*. These petty officers, having risen from the ranks, and invested with an authority for which they were often quite unsuited, were al-ways ready, for a consideration, to aid the cause of some aspiring politician, now on one side, now on another. They are now, fortunately, abolished.

The Spanish artillery is a splendid body, and is officered from the best families in the country. In the only military insurrection in which the common soldiers shot some of the officers obnoxious to them—that of the Montaño Barracks, in 1866—the leader of the mutinists was a certain *hidalgo*. It was the promotion of this man that led indirectly to the abdication of Don Amadeo, who opposed the action. Indignant at the disgrace to the service, all of the artillery officers in Spain sent in their resignations. They were accepted, and the *primo sargentos* raised to the rank of officers to fill their places. The result was unlimited mutiny among the rank and file and danger to the State. Some of the young officers who had retained their uniforms, though no longer attached to the corps, finding the troops in utter disorder and revolt, quietly donned their uniforms, went down to the barracks, and gave their orders. The men instantly fell into the ranks, and the situation was saved. The *primo sargentos* were abolished, the officers reinstated. But Amadeo had had enough; he ceased to attempt to reign constitutionally in a country where the constitution meant only one more form of personal greed and excess. He was *demasiado honesto* for the crew he had been called to command, and he left the country to tumble about in its so-called "republican" anarchy until another military *pronunciamiento* set Alfonso XII. on the throne. And that has been, fortunately, the last performance of a kind once so common in Spain.

All military men admire the effective corps of light mountain artillery. The small guns are carried on the backs of the splendid mules for which the Spanish army is famous, and can be taken up any mountain path which these singular animals can climb. Mules are also used to drag the heavier guns, and must be invaluable in a mountainous country. The animals are quite as large as ordinary horses, are lithe, active, and literally unhurtable. I have myself seen a mule, harnessed to a cart which was discharging stones over the edge of a deep pit, when levelling the ground at the end of the Fuente Castellana in Madrid, over-balanced by the weight behind him, fall over, turn a somersault in mid-air, cart and all, and, alighting thirty feet below, shake himself, ponder for a few seconds on the unexpected event in his day's labour, and then proceed to draw the cart, by this time satisfactorily emptied, out of the pit by the sloping track at the farther side, and continue his task absolutely unhurt and undisturbed.

Until the final overthrow of the Carlists by Alfonso XII., the Basque Provinces, amongst their most cherished *fueros*, were exempted from the hated conscription; but the victorious King made short work of that and of all other special rights and privileges—which, in truth, had been abused—and now all the country is subject to conscrip-

tion. Every man from nineteen to twenty years
of age is liable to serve in the ranks, except those
who are studying as officers. A payment of £60
frees them from service during peace; but if the
country is at war there is no exemption. The
conscripts are bound for twelve years—three with
the colours, three in the first reserve, three in
the second, and three in the third.

Navy? Alas! Spain has none. Two battle-
ships alone remain—*El Pelayo* and *Carlos V.* (the
former about nine thousand five hundred tons,
the latter not more than seven thousand)—and
some destroyers and torpedoes. How a nation
that once ruled the sea, and whose sailors trav-
ersed and conquered the New World, has allowed
her navy to become practically extinct at the moment when nations which have almost no seaboard
are trying to bring theirs up within measurable
distance of England's, it is impossible to say.
Even before the outbreak of the war with America there were but a few battle-ships, and these
were wanting in guns and in almost all that could
make them effective—save and except the men,
who behaved like heroes. It seems to be a con-
solation to Spaniards to remember that it was in
the pages of an English journal that an Englishman, who had seen the whole of the disastrous
war, wrote: " If Spain were served by her statesmen as she has been served by her navy, she
would be one of the greatest nations of the world
to-day."

The history of the part borne by the Spanish
navy in the late war with America, as written by
one of Admiral Cervera's captains,[1] with the
publication of the actual telegrams which passed
between the Government and the fleet, and the
military commanders in the colonies, is one of
the most heartrending examples of the sacrifice, not only of brave men, but of a country's
honour to political intrigue or the desire to retain
office.   This, at least, is the opinion of the writer
of this painful history, and his statements are
fully borne out by the original telegrams, since
published.   It is impossible to imagine that any
definite policy at all was followed by the advisers
of the Queen Regent in this matter, unless it
were the incredible one ascribed to it by Captain
Concas Palan of deliberately allowing the fleet,
such as it was, to be destroyed—in fact, in the
case of Admiral Cervera's squadron, sending it
out to certain and foreseen annihilation—so as to
make the disaster an excuse for suing for peace,
without raising such a storm at home as might
have upset the Ministry.   With both fleets sunk,
and those of their men not slain, prisoners of war,
there was no alternative policy but peace.   Captain Concas Palan claims for his chief and the
comrades who fell in this futile and disastrous
affair " a right to the legitimate defence which
our country expects from us, though it is against

[1] *La Escuadra del Almirante Cervera*, por Victor M.
Concas Palan.

the interested silence which those who were the cause of our misfortunes would fain impose on us," and says that "some day, and that probably much sooner than seems probable at present," the judgment of Spain on this episode will be that of the English *Review*, which he quotes as the heading of his chapter. He goes on: " War was accepted by Spain when the island of Cuba was already lost to her, and when the dispatch of a single soldier more from the Peninsula was infinitely more likely to have caused an insurrection than that of which our Ministers were afraid—at the moment, also, when our troops were in want of the merest necessaries, the arrears of pay being the chief cause of their debilitated condition, and when a great part of the Spanish residents in Cuba, under the name of ' Reformers,' 'Autonomists,' etc., had made common cause with the insurgents, while they were enriching themselves to a fabulous extent by contracts for supplies and transports. In these circumstances it was folly to accept a struggle with an immensely rich country, possessing a population four times that of ours, and but a pistol shot from the seat of action." The Government of Spain was perfectly aware that the troops in Cuba were already quite insufficient even to cope with the insurgents, that the people at home were already murmuring bitterly at the cost of the war, and that it was impossible to send out a contingent of any practical value. Sickness of all kinds, enteric, anæmia, and all the evils of under-fed and badly found troops, were rapidly consuming the forces in Cuba, '' and yet the Government took no thought of who was to man the guns whose gunners were drifting daily into the hospital and the cemetery. . . . The national debt was increasing in a fabulous manner, and recourse was had to the mediæval remedy of debasing the currency, while even at that moment the troops had more than a year's pay in arrear, and absolute penury was augmenting their other sufferings.''

This was the moment which the responsible Ministers of the Crown thought propitious to throw down the gauntlet to the overwhelming power of America rather than to face what the writer terms the '' cabbage-headed riff-raff of the Plaza de la Cevada '' of Madrid. Again and again was the absolute inefficiency of the fleet pointed out to them. Even the few ships there were, all of them vastly inferior to those of the United States' navy, were without their proper armament; they might have been of some service in defence of the coast of Spain, but in aggressive warfare they were useless. Allowing somewhat for the natural indignation of one of those who was sacrificed, who saw his beloved commander and his comrades-in-arms sent like sheep to the slaughter, and all for an idea,—and that a perfectly stupid and useless one,—there is no gainsaying the facts which Captain Concas Palan relates, and the original telegrams verify every word of his story.

Admiral Cervera was sent out with sealed orders; but he had done all that was in his power—even asking to be relieved of his command—to prevent the folly of sending away from the coasts of the mother country the only ships which could have protected her, while they were absolutely useless against the American navy in the Antilles. Left with no alternative but obedience, he managed to gain the safe harbour of Santiago de Cuba with his squadron intact. Secure from attack, he landed his men to assist in the defence of the town from the land side. And then came the incredible orders that he was to take out his four ships to be destroyed by the American navy waiting outside! Never in the world's history was a more magnificent piece of heroism displayed than in the obedience to discipline which caused Admiral Cervera to re-embark his marines and lead them forth to certain death, well knowing what they were to face, for he hid nothing from them. He called on them as sons of Spain, and they answered heroically, as Spaniards have ever done in history: " For honour! "

Spain has suffered deeply and sorely in her pride; but she has never worn her heart on her sleeve—she suffers in silence. A quotation from the *Época* of July 5th, two days after the destruction of Cervera's fleet, shows the spirit in which the country bore that terrible blow. It is headed " Hours of Agony." " Our grief to-day has nothing in it which was unexpected. The

13

laws of logic are invincible; our four ships could not by any possibility have escaped the formidable American squadron. The one thing that Spain expected of her sons was that they should perish heroically. They have perished! They have faced their destiny; they have realised the sole end which Spain looked for, in this desperate conflict into which she has been drawn by God knows what blind fatality; they have fallen with honour.''

That is true; but how about the leaders whose long misrule of the colonies had helped to bring on the disaster which their predecessors for many years had courted? How about the political corruption which, when large sums were being spent on the colonies, had allowed immense private fortunes to be made while Manila was left without defences, and the absolutely unassailable bay of Santiago de Cuba had on the fort which commanded its entrance only useless old guns of a past century, more likely to cause the death of those who attempted to serve them than to injure an enemy? How about the Government that deliberately entered on a war of which the end was perfectly foreseen, and, while seated safely in office at home, thought the '' honour of Spain '' sufficiently vindicated by offering up its navy, already made useless by neglect and niggardliness, as a sacrifice? Captain Concas Palan points out that even after it was fully recognised that the retention of Cuba was impossible, the worst catastrophes might have been avoided. "In place of treating for peace while the squadron was intact at Santiago, which, as well as Manila, could have been defended for some time, the Ministers waited to sue for peace until everything was lost, while it was perfectly well known beforehand that that result was inevitable." During the whole time, *mañana veremos* was the rule of action —a to-morrow that never was to dawn for those whose lives it was intended to sacrifice. Heaven works no miracles for those who fling themselves against the impossible!

So long ago as 1823, Thomas Jefferson wrote to President Monroe: "The addition of the island of Cuba to our Confederacy is exactly what is wanted to round our power as a nation to the point of its utmost interest." John Quincy Adams went so far as to state that "Cuba gravitates to the United States as the apple yet hanging on its native trunk gravitates to the earth which sustains it"—a statement which has the more force when it is remembered that for over fifty years the Cuban insurgents had been liberally supplied with arms, ammunition, stores, and troops from the United States whenever they required them! And this, not because Cuba was mismanaged by Spain, but because America coveted her as "the most interesting addition that could be made to our system of States," to quote Jefferson once more.

Nevertheless, the heroic sons of Spain were

offered up as an expiation for the sins of her political jugglers for generations past. With the knowledge that America had at least for seventy years been seeking an excuse for "rounding her power as a nation" by the seizure of Cuba, no real effort was made to redress the grievances of her native population, nor to efficiently defend her coasts.

The state of affairs in Manila was still worse. The culpable neglect of the Government had resulted in the so-called squadron not being possessed of one single ship of modern construction or armament; and when the unfortunate marines and their heroic commanders had been immolated by the overwhelming superiority in numbers and efficiency of the Americans, the noisy injustice and anger of a senseless crowd at home were allowed to compass the lasting disgrace of casting the blame for the foreseen disasters on Admiral Montojo, who was thrown as a victim to the jackals.

To-day, we find Spain absolutely without a navy. Two second- or third-class ships—and they not even properly found or armed—are all she possesses. Men she has, however, with the traditions of a great past, while the officers of her navy are thoroughly alive to the class of ships and the armament which are needed to give their country the protection, and their foreign policy the dignity, which other countries of far less importance are able to sustain. No wonder that her writers

are pointing out that instead of being satisfied
with immense long-winded despatches and notes,
couched in grandiloquent language, which Spanish Foreign Ministers seem to think amply sufficient, strong nations have a habit of sending an
iron-clad, or two or three cruisers to back up their
demands, and that no other European country
but Spain thinks it safe or wise to leave her coasts
and her commerce entirely without protection in
case of a European war breaking out. Will the
nation itself take the matter in hand, and in this,
as in so many other matters, advance in spite of
its Government? If it waits for the political seesaw by which both parties avoid responsibility,
there will be small chance of a navy. The same
ministry is in power to-day which landed the
country in the Spanish-American War, and it
would seem as if the nation considers it the best
it can produce. *Mañana veremos?*

CHAPTER XII

RELIGIOUS LIFE

THE natural bent of the Spanish mind is religious. Taking the nation as a whole, with all its marvellous variations in race and character, no portion of it has ever been reproached for insincerity in its religious beliefs. It has been often held up to reproach for bigotry and superstition; but the people have in past ages been penetrated by a sincere reverence for what they have believed to be religion, and perhaps no other nation has been more thoroughly imbued with an unwavering faith in the dogmas taught by its religious instructors. English Roman Catholics—especially those who have seceded from the Anglican Church—are fond of declaring that Spain is "a splendid Catholic country," " the home of true Catholicism," and so forth. To a certain extent this has been true of it in the past, and " dignity, loyalty, and the love of God " are still the ideals of the people at large, although in Spain, as in some other Continental nations, the practice of religious duties is now, to a great extent, left to the women of the family and to the

peasantry.   Young Spain, and the progressive
party in it, can no longer be said to be under the
domination of the Church, even in outward appearance.   It will be well if the swing of the
pendulum does not carry them very far from it,
and into open revolt.

The history of the Church in Spain and of its
relations with Rome is a curious one.   It can
scarcely be said to have been much more amenable
to the Papacy than that of the Church of England,
though it has remained always within the pale of
the Roman Catholic persuasion.   In the old time
the kings aspired to be the head of the Spanish
Church, and were none too subservient to the
Pope.   The Inquisition and the Society of Jesus
were distinctly Spanish, and not Roman, and
were at times actually at variance with the Vatican.   Probably from their long struggles with
the barbarians, and later with the Moors, Spaniards have a habit of always speaking of themselves as Christians rather than Catholics, which
strikes strangely on one's ears.

The evils which have been wrought in Spain
by the terrible incubus of the Inquisition, and by
the domination of the Jesuits and other orders,
who obtained possession of the teaching of youth,
have been little less than disastrous, because their
power has been deliberately used for ages past to
keep the lower classes in a state of absolute ignorance, slaves of the grossest superstition, and mere
puppets in the hands of the priesthood.   Even

well within the memory of living people it was thought a pity that women should be allowed to learn even to read and write,—safer to have them quite ignorant,—while the peasantry and the inferior classes believed anything they were told, and could be excited to any pitch of fanaticism by the preaching of their religious teachers. The Inquisition was often used as a political machine, and was sometimes only clothed with the semblance of religion; but by whomsoever it was directed, and for whatsoever purpose, it was a vile and soul-destroying institution. It deliberately ground down and destroyed every spark of intelligence, of liberty, of attempt at progress; it dominated the whole nation like the shadow of the upas tree, manufactured hypocrites, and led to the debasing of a naturally fine people of good instincts to an ignorant and fanatical mob, who, in the name of religion, were entertained with gigantic *autos-da-fé*, as the Roman populace were with the terrible spectacles of their gladiatorial shows and the immolation of Christian victims in the arena.

It was the people themselves who rose against this hateful tyranny; it was their better instincts that put an end to the " Holy Office " and its enormous crimes. Shortly after the Revolution of 1868, when religious liberty had been established, and the people, for the first time in their long history of disaster, were breathing the air of freedom, certain improvements which were being

made, in the shape of laying out new streets,
pulling down old rookeries, and building better
houses, led to a new road being cut through the
raised ground outside the Santa Barbara Gate.
The exact spot of the great *Quemadero*—the oven
of the Inquisition—was not known, but it chanced
that the workmen cut right through the very
centre of it. A more ghastly sight, or an object-
lesson of more potency, could scarcely be imagined. The Government of the day found it
advisable to cover it up as quickly as possible;
the excitement of the people was thought to be
dangerous; and though those at the head of
affairs were no friends to the priests or the
Jesuits, there was no desire to reawaken the
passions and let loose the vengeance which
led the populace in 1834 to murder them wholesale.

I happened to be returning from a ride with a
companion when, quite accidentally, we came
upon this excavation, and even passed down the
new road before we realised where we were.
The *Quemadero* had evidently been in the shape
of an immense basin. There in the banks at
each side were the stratified layers of human
ashes; between each *auto-da-fé* it was evident
that the remains had been covered with a thick
layer of earth; finally, at the top of all these
smaller bands of black, horrible ashes, came one
huge deposit, which marked the awful scene
of the last gigantic *auto*. This ghastly bonfire

was sixty feet square, and seven feet high, as history records, when one hundred and five victims were slowly tortured to a frightful death in the name of Christ, while the King, Charles II., and his Court and the howling rabble of Madrid looked on with savage enjoyment. Nothing can ever obliterate the impression of that scene, nor make one forget the deadly clinging of those ghastly black ashes, which the wind scattered about, and which it was impossible to escape or to get rid of. The fell work of the " religious " authors of the holocaust had been well done— nothing was left but ashes; and the next day, by order of the Government, sand or soil had been thrown over all that could bear witness to this horrible episode in the history of the Church in Spain, while the people who inhabit the houses built over the spot probably know nothing of the records of human agony and brutal bigotry that still lie beneath their homes.

We hear of these things and read of them in history, but one needs to have seen that awful memorial to realise what share the Inquisition has had in transforming a naturally heroic and kindly people into the inert masses which nothing, or almost nothing, would move so long as they had *pan y toros* (bread and bulls). Thanks to the horrors of the Inquisition and the *Autos-da-fé*, the whole people have acquired a character which assuredly they do not deserve. The blind bigotry and cynical cruelty of Philip II. and his lunatic successors have been identified with the races over which, unfortunately for Spain, they ruled for so many years. When one remembers that this is the view taken of the Inquisition, and of the domination of the Church in effacing all kinds of culture, by the liberal and educated Spaniard of to-day, and that there is, even now, an extreme party which would fain see the " Holy Office " re-established, with all its old powers, it is easy to understand at what a critical point the clerical question has arrived in Spain; nor need one wonder at the feeling which in all parts of the kingdom has been aroused by the recrudescence of the religious orders, more especially of the de-termined struggle of the Jesuits to retain and even to reassert their power.

The Madonna, who is always spoken of as " La Vírgen," never as " Santa María," is the great object of love and of reverence in Spain, while the words *Dios* and *Jesus* are used as common ex-clamations in a way that impresses English people rather unfavourably. It is a shock to hear all classes using the *Por Dios !* which with us is a mark of the purest blackguardism, and the use as common names of that of Our Lord and of *Salva-dor*, or Saviour, always strikes a disagreeable note. There is in Madrid a " Calle Jesus," and the sacred name, used as a common expletive, is heard on all sides. One of the most charming of Yradier's Andalusian songs, addressed by a *con-trabandista* to his *novia*, runs thus:

Pero tengo unas patillas.
Que patillas puñála !
Es lo mejor que se ha jecho
En de Jesu Cristo acá ! [1]

And no one is offended; in fact, no irreverence is probably meant.

But the innumerable "Vírgenes" which abound throughout the country, and all seem different, have the heartfelt devotion of all classes. To one or other of them the bull-fighter goes for protection and aid before he enters the arena; the mother whose child lies sick vows her magnificent hair to the Virgin of the Atocha, or of the Pillar, or some of the many others scattered about the country, if only she will grant what she asks; and you may see these marvellous locks, tied with coloured ribbons, hanging amongst the motley assemblage of votive offerings by the side of her altar, when the prayer has been answered. It is difficult for us, with the best intentions, not to let prejudice colour our judgment, and to understand what we are told — that these are really all the same " Mother of God "; for, if so, one would imagine that she would hear the devout prayers of her worshippers, to whichever of the wooden images—most of them said to have been carved by St. Luke, and black by age, if not by nature—they are addressed. But no, the Vir-

[1] " But I have such a stunning pair of whiskers !
The best that have ever been seen since those of
Jesus Christ ! "

gen del Cármen is only efficacious in certain circumstances; and in the time of Isabel II. she used to be taken down from her altar and placed in the Queen's bedroom whenever an addition to the Royal Family was imminent. Those in the other parts of Spain have each their specialty, and pilgrimages are necessary to their shrines before the prayers addressed to them can be listened to by the original.

The various saints in their way are wooed with candles burnt before their images, or little altars set up to them at home; but they are sometimes treated with scant courtesy if they do not answer the expectations of their worshippers. On one occasion in Madrid, I remember, San Isidro, who is the patron of the labouring classes, had the bad taste, as his votaries considered, to send rain on his own *fiesta*—a thing unknown before. Lest he should err in this way again, the mob went to his church, at that time the principal one in Madrid, smashed the windows, and did all the damage they could compass before the Civil Guards came to the rescue. A servant-girl I knew, had for a long time been praying to San Antonio to send her a *novio* (sweetheart), expending money in tapers, and otherwise trying to propitiate the saint. At last, finding him deaf to all entreaties, she took the little wooden image she had bought, tied a string round his neck, and hung him in the well, saying: "You shall stop there till you send me what I want." Some little time after, she actually found a *novio*, and hastened gratefully to take San Antonio out of his damp quarters, set him up on his altar again, and burn tapers for his edification. I had thought this an example of special ignorance and superstition; but the other day, in reading some of the papers of the *Spanish Folklore Library*, I found there is a widespread belief that if San Antonio, and probably some other saints, do not answer the prayers of their votaries who burn candles before them, it is a good thing to hang them in a well till they come to their senses! It is difficult for any unbiassed person to understand that this is not fetish worship, as it would certainly seem to be, but we are told that it is something quite different.

The religious *fiestas*, as I have said, may be classed among the amusements of the people. During the warm season they invariably end with a bull-fight. In winter there are no bulls. Whether it be the *Romería* of Santiago de Compostelo, the *Santa Semana* in Toledo or Seville, *Noche-Buena* and the *Day of the Nativity* in Madrid or Barcelona, gaiety and enjoyment seem to be the order of the day. Even Lent is not so bad, for just before it comes the Carnival and the grotesque "Burial of the Sardine" by the *gente bajo*, and of the three great masked balls, one is given in mid-Lent, to prevent the Lenten ordeal being too trying, and Holy Thursday is always a *fiesta* and day of enjoyment. On this day, in Madrid, takes place the washing of the feet of the poor in the Royal Palace—a function that savours a good deal of the ridiculous, but which was never omitted by the *piadosa* Isabel II., and was revived by her son. For forty-eight hours the bells of all the churches remain silent, no vehicles are allowed in the streets, which are gravelled along the routes Royalty will take to visit on foot seven of the churches, where the Holy Sepulchres are displayed; and in the afternoon all Madrid resorts to the Plaza del Sol and the Carrera San Geronimo, to show off their gayest costumes in a regular gala promenade. Finally, on Saturday morning—why forty-eight hours only is allowed for the supposed entombment does not quite appear—the bells clang forth, noise and gaiety pervade the whole city, and the day ends with a cock-fight and the reopening of the theatres, and the first grand bull-fight of the season is held on Easter Sunday. Verily, the Church is mindful of the weakness of its vassals, and shows as much indulgence as is thought needful to keep the people amused and careless of all else. I remember, when I first noticed this wearing of the most gaudy colours on Maundy Thursday, a day one would naturally expect to be one of special mourning, I was told it was allowed by the Church because on that day Pilate put the purple robe on Our Lord!

The processions and functions of Holy Week and other *fiestas* have been so often and so fully described that there is no need to refer to them;

but there are several curious survivals and religious customs in out-of-the-way places which
seem to have escaped notice. I have not been
able to find in any book on Spain a description of
the strange dance which takes place in the cathedral of Seville on, I think, three days in the year,
of which two are certainly the day of the Virgin
and that of Corpus Christi. The origin of the
dance seems to be lost, nor is its special connection with Seville known. All that one can hear
of it is that one of the archbishops of Toledo
objected to the dance as being irreverent and unusual, and ordered it to be stopped. The indignant people referred the matter to the Pope, but
even the date of this appeal seems to be dubious,
if not unknown. His Holiness replied that he
could not judge of the matter unless he himself
saw the dance. Accordingly, the boys who
figure in this strange performance were taken
to Rome, and they solemnly danced before the
Pope. His verdict was that there was nothing
irreverent about the dance, but he thought, as it
was known only to Seville, it would be better
eventually to discontinue it; but so long as the
dress worn on the occasions when it is practised,
lasted, the dance might continue. The dresses
have lasted to the present day, and will always
continue to last, say the Sevillanos, for as one part
wears out it is renewed, but never a whole gar-
ment made. The dress is peculiar: it consists of
short trousers to the knees, and a jacket which

hangs from one shoulder, stockings and shoes with large buckles or bows, and a soft hat, somewhat of the shape of a Tam-o'-shanter, with one feather—that of an eagle, I think. The dress is red and white for the day of Corpus, and blue and white for the day of the Virgin, covered with the richest gold embroidery, for which Spain has always been famous. The boys, holding castanets in each hand, advance, dancing with much grace and dignity, until they reach the front of the High Altar; there they remain, striking their castanets and performing slow and very graceful evolutions for some time, gradually retiring again as they came in, dancing, down the nave. The boys are regularly instructed in the dance by the priests, and the number is kept up, so that neither dancers nor garments ever fail. The Pope's order is obeyed, while the Sevillanos retain their strange religious function. The fact of the performance taking place in the evening perhaps accounts for its being so little known, but it would seem also as if the authorities of the cathedral do not care to have attention drawn to it. The dance is called *los seises*, and even the origin of the name is unknown.

In Holy Week and at Christmas are performed passion plays at some of the theatres, strangely realistic, and sometimes rousing the audience to wild indignation, especially against Judas Iscariot, who is hissed and hooted, and is often the recipient of missiles from the spectators, while interspersed

14

with this genuine feeling one hears shouts of laughter when anything occurs to provoke it. On one occasion one of the Roman soldiers (always unpopular in the religious processions) appeared on the stage, dragging, by a cord round the neck, a miserable-looking man carrying a huge cross, so heavy that it caused him continually to fall. As the soldier kicked him up again, and continued to drag him along by the neck, the audience became ungovernable in their rage. "*Déjale! Déjale! Bruto! Bruto!*" they yelled; and, finally threatening to storm the stage and immolate the offending soldier, the play had to be stopped and the curtain rung down.

In villages too poor to possess *pasos*—the beautifully modelled life-size figures which form the *tableaux* in the rich churches and processions—human actors take their place. In Castellon de la Plana, where there is a yearly procession in honour of Santa María Magdalena, somewhat curious scenes take place. The Magdalen, in the days of her sin, is acted by a girl chosen for her beauty, but not for her character. She is gorgeously attired, and is allowed to retain her dress and ornaments after the performance. She is installed in state in a cart decorated with palms and flowers, and is surrounded by all the men of the village on foot, for it is part of the performance that they are allowed to say what they please to her. She acts the part to perfection apparently, and enjoys it, to boot. In another car comes the penitent Magdalen, dressed in pure white, and decorated with flowers. This part may be taken only by a young girl of unblemished character. It is thought the greatest honour that can be paid to her, and you are told by the people that she is always married within the year. This procession winds its way up the mountain to a small shrine of Santa María Magdalena, where it is said that her church once stood; but finding the climb up the hill was inconvenient to the lame and the aged, she very considerately, one night, moved the whole edifice down intact to Castellon de la Plana, where it now stands.

Going by rail once, many years ago, to Toledo, to see the processions on Good Friday, the train was accidentally delayed for some time a little distance from one of the stations, and there, in a small garden by the roadside, was being enacted the scene of the Crucifixion by human actors. A full-size cross was erected, and on it, apparently, hung a man crowned with thorns, and with head bowed upon his breast. In reality he was kneeling on two ledges placed for the purpose at a convenient distance from the cross-bars. It was cold, and the actor was covered by an old brown tattered cloak, such as the peasants wear now, and which we see in Velasquez's pictures. His feet stuck out behind the cross, but his arms were tied in a position which must soon have become painful. Around lay a cock tied by his legs, a ladder, a sponge tied on a stick, a sword, a lantern, and all the usual emblems of the Passion. The holy women and the Roman soldiers with their spears were just coming out of the cottage hard by to take up their positions in this strange and pathetic *tableau*. The face of that peasant in the tattered brown cloak, not less than the spectacle of the people kneeling around in evident sorrow and worship, haunted me for many a day.

CHAPTER XIII

EDUCATION AND THE PRIESTHOOD

EDUCATION, especially that of the masses, has made great strides since the Revolution. At that time perfect liberty of religion and of instruction was established, and in this particular the somewhat retrograde movement at the Restoration, in allowing the return of the religious orders banished in the early years of the century, has only resulted in a greater number of private schools being established by the Jesuits and other teaching orders. With the public instruction they have never been allowed to interfere.

Every town and village has now its municipal and free schools, kept up by the *Diputacion provincial*. In all the chief towns there are technical and arts and crafts schools, also free, the expenses being borne by the Ministry of Fomento. Besides these are many private schools, taught by Jesuits and other teaching orders. The Ministry of Fomento is at present trying to bring in a law making education compulsory, and bringing all schools under State control. There are numerous girls' schools, managed by committees of ladies, as well as the convent schools and other private establishments. There are also normal schools, maintained by the Ministry of Fomento, where women and girls, as well as men, can take degrees and gain certificates for teaching purposes. In every capital of Spain one of these schools is established. There are ten universities, of which the principal is that of Madrid. In some of these only medicine and law are studied, but others are open for every class of learning. In all these numerous schools and colleges great advance has been made in late years; in the department of science, electricity has taken a very noticeable step forward, and in applied electricity Spain probably compares favourably with any of the European nations. Even the small towns and some villages are lighted by electricity, having gone straight from petroleum to electric light. Most of the large towns have, besides the light, electric tramways, telephones, etc., the engineers and artisans employed in these works being of a very high class. Electrical engineers are not under Government control, as the civil and mechanical engineers are, and have therefore better chances of coming to the front and making a career for themselves. The Government engineers, however, are kept up to the mark of other countries, and an attempt has been made by the present Minister to alter the system by which civil and mechanical engineers are compulsorily a body appointed and controlled by Government.

Medical science has made great strides during the last ten or twelve years. The hospitals are reformed, and all sanitary and antiseptical arrangements are now strictly attended to, and brought into line with the latest developments of science. A fine new hospital, San Juan de Dios, has been built in Madrid, on the plan of St. Thomas's in London, and this is only one of many improvements. The reorganisation of all scientific teaching is now engaging the attention of the Minister. An excellent sign of the present state of medical science in Spain—which only a few years ago was so far behind the age—is the fact that the International Congress of Medicine is fixed to meet in Madrid, for the first time, in 1902.

Since the establishment of religious liberty, the Americans seem to have made themselves very busy in missionary work. Mrs. Gulick, the wife of the American missionary in San Sebastian, claims to have " proved the intellectual ability of Spanish girls," and has secured State examination and recognition of her pupils by the National Institution of San Sebastian, and a few have even obtained admission to the examinations of the Madrid University, where they maintained a high rank. One always has a feeling that missionaries might easily find a field for their zealous labours in their own country; but if an impulse was needed from a foreign people for the initiation of a higher education among the daughters of Spain, they will certainly be able to carry on the work themselves, with such women as Emelia Pardo Bazan to lead the way. Mrs. Gulick is said to project a college for women in Madrid without distinction of creed. The whole affair sounds a little condescending, as though America were coming to the aid of a nation of savages; but if the Spaniards themselves do not object, no one else has any right to do so.

The Protestant movement has made but little progress in Spain. The religion is scarcely fitted to the genius of the people, and the Anglican Church has shown no desire to proselytise a nation which has as much right to its own religious opinions and form of worship as the English nation. The Americans and English Nonconformists are very busy, however, and talk somewhat largely of the results of their labours. In most of the large towns there are English chapels and schools, and a certain number among the lower classes of Spaniards have joined these communities. A private diary of a visit to Madrid so long ago as 1877 describes the English service there. The congregation numbered "quite five hundred." "They were of the poorer classes of both sexes, with a sprinkling of well-dressed men and women. They seemed to perform their devotions in a spirit of entire reverence and piety, not unlike a similar class in our churches at home. The clergyman delivered an impressive and forcible discourse, chiefly on the honour due to the name of God, and reprobated the profane use of the most sacred names, so common among the Spanish people. . . . Altogether I look upon the congregation at the Calle de Madera as a nucleus of genuine Protestantism in Spain."

As this is the opinion of a perfectly unbiassed onlooker, and has nothing of the professional element about it, it may be taken as absolutely reliable. In the towns, such as Bilbao, where there is a large English colony, there are various churches and chapels, and considerable numbers of communicants and Sunday scholars. Looking back, as I am able to do, to the days when there was no toleration for an alien faith; when even Christian burial for the "heretic" was quite a new thing, and living people could tell of the indignities heaped on the corpse of any unlucky English man or woman who died in "Catholic" Spain; when to have omitted, or even hesitated about, any of the religious actions imposed by the Church would have exposed one to gross insult, and perhaps injury; the progress towards enlightened toleration of the opinions of others seems to have been remarkable. It is, perhaps, more significant that the members of the new congregations should be generally of the lower classes, because it is precisely these people who have always been mere unthinking puppets in the hands of their priests.

Although there is at the present moment such a deep and widespread revolt against the Jesuits and some of the other orders, especially among the students and the better class of artisans and workmen, there is not, so far as a stranger may judge, a revolt against the Church itself, nor even against the parochial clergy. It would seem rather that there is a fixed determination that the priests shall keep to their business, that of the service of religion, and shall not be allowed to interfere in secular education, or, by use of the confessional, to dominate the family; and, above all, that the convents shall not be filled by force, undue persuasion, or cajolery. The state of the Roman Catholic religion and its priesthood in England is constantly being held up as the ideal of what the Church in Spain should be.

Almost all the modern novelists of Spain show us characters of priests with whom every reader must feel sympathy. Valera, Galdós, Pardo Bazan, and others depict individual clerics who are simple, straightforward, pious, and in every way worthy men, the friend of the young and the helper of the sorrowful. Sometimes they are not very learned, and not at all worldly-wise, but they show that the type is largely represented amongst the priesthood of Spain, and there are not wanting some of distinctly liberal tendencies. There was a remarkable article in a Madrid paper of radical, if not socialistic, tendencies, the other day, by one who signed himself "A priest of the Spanish Catholic Church." Lamenting over the sentimentalism of modern religion, and the distance it had travelled from its old models, he says: " Instead of the Vírgen being held up to admiration as the Mother of Our Lord, and as an example of all feminine perfection, the ideal woman and mother, the people are called on to worship the idea of the Immaculate Conception, an abstract dogma of recent invention, and in place of showing us the perfect man in the Son of God, they are asked to worship a ' bleeding heart,' abstracted from the body, and held up as an object of reverence, apart from the living body of Jesus Christ." It is the reform of the national religion still ardently loved in spite of all the crimes that have been committed in her name, that the liberal-minded Spaniard wants, not the substitution of a foreign church; although no doubt the opportunity, now for the first time possible, of learning that there are people every whit as good and earnest as themselves, who yet hold religious opinions other than theirs, is bound to have a widening and softening effect on the narrowness of a creed which has hitherto been regarded as the only one.

The extraordinary outbreak against the Jesuits and the religious orders of the last year had many causes, and had probably long been seething, and waiting for something to open the floodgates. That something came in the marriage of the Princess of Asturias, and the coincidence, accidental or otherwise, of the production of Galdós's play of *Electra*. The marriage was a love match;

the two young sons of the Count of Caserta, who were nephews of the Infanta Isabel on her husband's side, had been constantly at the Palace in Madrid, companions of the boy King. An attachment sprang up between Don Carlos, the elder of the two, and the King's elder sister, the Princess of Asturias. In every way the projected marriage was obnoxious to the people. The Count of Caserta himself had been chief of the staff to the Pretender, Don Carlos, and though he and his sons had taken the oath of allegiance to the young King, Spaniards have learned to place little reliance on such oaths. Had not Montpensier sworn allegiance to his sister-in-law Isabel II.? and of how much was it worth when the time came that he thought he could successfully conspire against her? To allow the heiress to the Crown to marry a Carlist seemed the surest way to reopen civil war, and upset the dynasty once more. Moreover, the Jesuits were supposed to be behind it all. The Apostolic party was apparently scotched and Carlism dead, but was not this one more move of the hated Jesuits to resuscitate both? The Liberal Government refused to allow the marriage; the Queen Regent, actuated, it is said, solely by the desire to secure what she considered the happiness of her daughter, who refused to give up her lover, was obstinate; and rather than give in, Sagasta and his Ministers resigned. A Conservative Ministry was formed— the methods of manipulating elections must be borne in mind—and the marriage was carried out. Even before the wedding-day the storm broke, and things looked ugly enough. Riots and disturbances occurred all over the country, as well as in Madrid itself; attacks were made on the houses of the Jesuits, who were credited with being the authors of the situation; and then followed the Government's suicidal step of suspending the constitutional guarantees over the whole country. Absolutism had once more raised its head! The Conservative Ministers, or many of them, were accused of being mere tools in the hands of the Jesuits, and it was complained that the confessor of the young King was one of the hated order.

For a time Spain seemed to be on the verge of one of her old convulsions. It appeared doubtful if the Queen Regent had not sacrificed the crown of one child to gratify the obstinacy of another. Fortunately, a catastrophe was averted. After vain efforts to retain the Conservative party in power, or to form a coalition, which all the best public men refused to join, Sagasta was once more recalled to power, the constitutional guarantees were restored, and the sharp crisis passed. But the attention of the nation had been attracted to what it considered the machinations of the Jesuits; order was indeed restored in Madrid and the provinces, but the "clerical question" had come to the front, and there was no possibility of allowing it to slumber again. It was discovered that not only had many of the religious orders, whose return had been allowed by convention after the Restoration, under certain limitations, largely increased their numbers beyond the limits allowed them, but that others had established themselves without any authorisation from the Government; also that considerable properties were being acquired in the country by the orders, though, of course, held under other names. The Chamber of Commerce and Industry of Madrid petitioned the Government to order an inquiry into the affairs of these religious bodies, pointing out that they were establishing manufactories of shoes, chocolate, fancy post-cards, and other objects of commerce, interfering with the ordinary trades, and underselling them, because, under the plea of being charitable institutions, they evaded duty. The heads of colleges and the Society of Public Teachers also asked for Government interference and the reassertion of the laws of 1881 and 1895, guaranteeing perfect liberty of instruction, because they affirmed that the Fathers, Jesuit and others, undermined the teaching of science in the schools by means of tracts distributed to the pupils, and also by using the power they obtained in the confessional to set aside the lessons in science given in the colleges.

The action of the Government was prompt and judicious. Strict inquiries were at once made into the question of the manufacturing orders, and those not paying the duty were reminded of the immediate necessity of doing so, and of

furnishing to the Ministry of Fomento full par-
ticulars of the trades carried on by them.   Houses
that were permitted by convention were warned
to reduce their numbers to those allowed by law,
and all unauthorised orders were warned at once
to leave the country.   The Press took a dignified and moderate position in the matter.   It
pointed out that perfect religious liberty existed,
and that all that was needful was to see that the
religious orders obeyed the law of the country as
other people did; but that to inaugurate a system
of persecution would be to return to the Dark
Ages, and to follow the bad example set by the
Church itself in former years.

Meanwhile, a clear intimation had been given
by the Government that public instruction was
absolutely free, and that no interference would
be allowed with the teaching of science in the
public schools.   After all, public opinion alone
can deal with the question of the confessional and
the occult influence of the priest, for the remedy
lies in the hands of those who place themselves
under the domination of the confessor.

So far, well!   The riots were at an end, and
the more sensible and law-abiding people were
satisfied that the ground stealthily gained by the
Jesuits had been cut from under their feet as soon
as the full light of day had been let in on their
proceedings.   Then came the extraordinary excitement caused by Galdós's play.   To a stranger
reading it, it is obvious that the public mind must

have been in a strange condition of alarm and distrust to have had such an effect produced upon it by a drama which has no great literary worth, and which appears commonplace and harmless to an outsider. The story is simply that of a young orphan girl, who, according to Spanish ideas, is extremely unconventional, though nothing worse. There is nothing of the emancipated young woman about her as the type is known in England; in fact, she has a perfect genius for those domestic virtues which "advanced" English women regard with disdain. The villain of the piece, is a certain Don Salvador, who, though the fact is never mentioned, is obviously a Jesuit, and the interest of the play consists in the efforts made by this man, first by fair means and then by foul, to separate Electra from her *fiancé*, and immure her in a convent. He succeeds, to all appearance, by at last resorting to an infamous lie, which reduces the girl to a state of insanity, in which she flies to the convent from the lover whom she has been led to believe is her own brother. Finally, by the action of a nun who leaves the convent at the same time as Electra, the truth is made known, and the girl is rescued.

"You fly from me, then?" exclaims Don Salvador.

"It is not flight, it is resurrection!" replies the lover, in the last words of the play.

This drama ran an unprecedented number of nights in Madrid, over fifteen thousand copies of the book were sold in a few weeks, and it is still running in the provinces. Some of the bishops and the superior clergy have had the folly to denounce the play and to forbid their congregations to witness or to read it. There is not an objectionable word or idea in it from first to last, except such as may be disagreeable to the Church— as that women should be educated so as to be the intellectual companions of their husbands, and should not be entrapped into convents by foul means and against their will. The action taken by the clergy in this matter has not only largely advertised the play, but has led to angry demonstrations against them, and has strengthened the temper of the people to resist all clerical domination in temporal matters.

There have not been wanting from time to time signs, especially in the large manufacturing towns, of a spirit of revolt against all religion. Socialism, atheism, and even anarchism are all in the air, and if these are to be counteracted by religious teaching at all, it will certainly not be by the narrow dogmatism of the old school. There is a deep fund of religious feeling in the Spanish character which it would take a great deal to uproot, but it must be a wide-spirited and enlightened faith which will retain its hold over the people, who are everywhere breaking their old bonds and thinking for themselves.

15

CHAPTER XIV

PHILANTHROPY—POSITION OF WOMEN—
MARRIAGE CUSTOMS

TRAVELLERS complain somewhat bitterly of
the increase in the numbers and the impor-
tunity of beggars in Spain; but wherever monks
abound, beggars also abound, and the long-unac-
customed sight of the various religious habits
naturally brings with it the hordes of miserable
objects who afford opportunities for the faithful to
exercise what they are taught to believe is charity
—loved of God. This, however, is more especially
the case in Granada, or those favoured spots
affected by the rich tourist, who has not always
the same opinion about indiscriminate charity as
the native Spaniard. In old days, the wise policy
of Charles III. had reduced very greatly the swarm
of beggars. A certain number of terrible-looking
objects — the fortunate possessors of withered
limbs, sightless eyeballs, or other disqualifications
for honest work — still ostentatiously displayed
their badges of professional mendicancy, and
lived, apparently quite comfortably, on the alms
of the passers-by. But the enormous competition

which has since sprung up in this " career " must interfere a good deal with its lucrativeness.

There is no poor law as yet in Spain. Philanthropy is left to voluntary effort; but the list of charities is so great, and so widely spread over the whole country, that one would think wholesale beggary would be superfluous. Madrid is divided into thirty-three parishes, each having a board of *Beneficéncias*, the Government holding a fund which these boards administer. The Queen is the President of the whole. Each board has its president and vice-president—generally ladies of the aristocracy—a treasurer, vice-treasurer, secretary, and vice-secretary, and a body of visitors; accounts are rendered monthly to the governing board, whose vice-president presides in the name of the Queen. There are also the confraternities of St. Vincent and St. Paul, the members of which are gentlemen and ladies who work independently of each other. These, however, have no established funds, but depend on voluntary subscriptions and gifts. Both these associations visit the poor in their own homes. The Pardo and the San Bernadino are societies and homes for benefiting men, women, and children; they have been founded by ladies. For boys there is the School of the Sacred Heart, and the Christian Brothers. The School of San Ildefonso belongs to the *Ayuntamiento*, and has secular masters. There is a small asylum, with chaplaincy attached, for architects. Santa Rita is a reformatory for boys in

Carabanchel, under a religious brotherhood. For girls there is the Horfino, the Mercédes Asylum —founded in memory of and kept up by the rents of Queen Mercédes—Santa Isabel and San Ilde-fonso, the French St. Vincent de Paul, San Blas, on the same lines as the Mercédes, Santa Cruz, the Inclusa, and the Spanish Vincent de Paul. For fallen girls there are the Adorers of the Blessed Sacrament, the Ladies of the Holy Trinity, and the Oblates of the Holy Redeemer.

In all parts of the country branches of these or similar institutions abound. None are more lib-eral to the funds of these voluntary charities than the bull-fighters, who, if they make large for-tunes, never forget the class from which they sprang, and are most generous in their donations. When occasion demands an extra effort, a *fiesta* is given at the Plaza de Toros, and the whole of the profits go to the charity for which it has been held. No doubt these schemes have their faults in operation, and Galdós in some of his popular novels does not fail to hold up—not exactly for admiration—the fashionable ladies who think it " smart," as we should say, to join these boards and societies, and talk with much unction of their public good works and the statistics of their pet societies, while neglecting the poor and the needy at their own doors, or trying to send into " Homes " those who have no desire or need to go there if a little Christian charity were only shown them by their neighbours. Nevertheless,

there is a large amount of organised philanthropy
in Spain to-day, and it appears to be of a wise and
efficient kind.   One should not forget to mention
also the workshops for the lowest orders, established by the Salerian Fathers, to which the attention of the Government has been called by late
events.

The general position of women in Spain and
their influence on public life cannot be described as of an advanced order.   As a rule, they
take no leading part in politics, devoting themselves chiefly to charitable works, such as those
already named.   There is, as we have seen, a
general movement for higher education and
greater liberty of thought and action amongst
women, and there is a certain limited number who
frankly range themselves on the side of so-called
"emancipation," who attend socialistic and other
"meetings"—a word which has now been form-
ally admitted into the Spanish language—and who
aspire to be the comrades of men rather than their
objects of worship or their playthings.   But this
movement is scarcely more than in its infancy.
It must be remembered that even within the
present generation the bedrooms allotted to girls
were always approached through that of the
parents, that no girl or unmarried woman could
go unattended, and that to be left alone in the
room with a man was to lose her reputation.
Already these things seem to be dreams of the
past; nor could one well believe, what is however

a fact, that there were fathers of the upper classes in the first half of the last century who preferred that their daughters should not learn to read or write, especially the latter, as it only enabled them to read letters clandestinely received from lovers and to reply to them. The natural consequence of this was the custom, which so largely prevailed, of young men, absolutely unknown to the parents, establishing correspondence or meetings with the objects of their adoration by means of a complaisant *doncella* with an open palm, or the pastime known as *pelando el pavo* (literally plucking the turkey), which consisted of serenades of love-songs, amorous dialogues, or the passage of notes through the *reja* — the iron gratings which protect the lower windows of Spanish houses from the prowling human wolf— or from the balconies. Many a time have I seen these interesting little missives being let down past my balcony — how trustful the innocents were! — to the waiting gallant below, and his drawn up. Only once I saw a neighbour, in the balcony below, intercept the post, and I believe substitute some other letter. Cruel sport!

Perhaps born of this necessity of making acquaintance by fair means or foul comes the custom, which appears to savour of such grossly bad manners to us, of a man making audible remarks on the appearance of a girl he has never seen before as she passes him in the street. *Ay! que buenos ojos! Que bonita eres! Que gracia tienes!*

and the like. Far from giving offence, the fair
one goes on her way, perhaps vouchsafing one
glance from those lovely eyes of hers, with only a
sense that her charms have received their due
tribute—not much elated, perhaps, but certainly
by no means offended; nor, indeed, was offence
intended. The fixed stare, which to us would
mean mere ill-bred ignorance, is only another
ordinary tribute to the passing fair one from the
other sex.

Marriage customs have changed much in the
last few decades, and even civil marriages are
now not wholly unknown. In old days, if the
ceremony was performed in church, the bride and
all the ladies must be attired in black, for which
reason the fashionable world established marriages in the house, where more brilliant costumes
might be displayed. These generally take place
in the evening, and the newly married couple do
not leave the house, unless the new home happens
to be close by. In any case, honeymoon tours are,
or were, unusual. The *velada* is the ceremony in
church, which must take place before the first
child is born, to legalise the marriage, but it does
not necessarily immediately follow the other ceremony. At it the ring is given. When the two
ceremonies take place at the same time it must be
in the morning, because the bride and bridegroom
partake of the Holy Sacrament fasting. From
the description of a *boda* in Galicia, in one of
Pardo Bazan's novels, it would seem that the

bride there wears white; even at the church. The wedding is a portentous affair, lasting all day from early morning, and the bride and bridegroom remain in the house. Fernan Caballero devotes some pages in *Clemencia* to showing how preferable is the Spanish custom of " remaining among friends " to that of the newly married couple, as she says, " exposing themselves to the jeers of postilions and stable-boys." Yet the English custom is in fact gaining ground, even in conservative Spain.

Although marriages are often made up by the parents and guardians, as in France, without any freedom on the part of the bride at least, custom or law gives the Spanish woman much more power than even in England. A girl desiring to escape from a marriage repugnant to her can claim protection from a magistrate, who will even, if necessary, take her out of her father's custody until she is of age and her own mistress. More than that, if a girl determines to marry a man of whom her parents disapprove, she has only to place herself under the protection of a magistrate to set them at defiance, nor have they the power to deprive her of the share of the family property to which by Spanish law she is entitled. I do not know if these things are altered now,—one does not hear so much of them,—but I know of several cases where daughters have been married from the magistrate's house against the wishes of their parents. In one case, the first intimation a father

received of his daughter's engagement was the
notice from a neighbouring magistrate that she
was about to be married, and in another, a daughter left her mother's house and was married from
that of the magistrate to a man without any in-
come and considerably below her in rank. In all
these cases, the contracting parties were of the
upper classes.

While on this subject, I must mention what
seems to us the barbarous manner in which infants are clothed and brought up, though the
English fashions of baths, healthy clothing, and
suitable food are now largely followed amongst
the upper classes. When the King was still an
infant a great deal of his clothing came from
England, and he was brought up in the English
method. This probably set the fashion, and the
little ones playing in the Park now are much like
those one is accustomed to see in London. But
among the poor, and even some of the bourgeois
class, the old insane customs prevail, and it is
not surprising to hear that the death-rate among
infants is extraordinarily high. From its birth
the poor child is tightly wrapped in swaddling
clothes, confining all its limbs, so that it presents
the appearance of a mummy, swathed in coarse
yellow flannel, only its head appearing. So stiffly
are they rolled up that I have seen an infant only
a few weeks old propped up on end against the
wall, or in a corner, while the mother was busy.
There is a superstition, too, about never washing

a child's head from the day it is born. The result is really indescribable. When it is about two
years old, a scab, which covers the whole head,
comes off of its own accord, and after that the
head may be cleansed without fear of evil consequences. Some English servants who have married in Spain set the example of keeping their
infants clean, and, therefore, healthy, from the
first, and, seeing the difference in the appearance
of the children, a few Spanish women have followed suit; but it requires a good deal of courage
to break away from old traditions and set one's
face against the sacred superstitions of ages—and
the mother-in-law!

One wonders, not that Spanish men grow bald
so early, and not bald only, but absolutely hair-
less, but that they ever have any hair at all; for
after all the troubles of their infancy their heads
are regularly shaved, or the hair cut off close to
the skin all the summer. On the principle of
cutting off the heads of dandelions as soon as they
appear, as a way of exterminating them, the surprising thing is that the hair does not become too
much discouraged even to try to sprout again.
Funny little objects they look, with only a dark
mark on the skin where the hair ought to grow
in summer, and at most a growth about as long
as velvet in the winter, until they are quite big
boys! The girls generally wear their hair so
tightly plaited, as soon as it is long enough to allow of plaiting at all, that they can scarcely close

their eyes. Young Spanish women, however, have magnificent hair; though they, too, grow bald when they are old, in a way that is never seen in England.

CHAPTER XV

MUSIC, ART, AND THE DRAMA

ONE is apt to forget how much the history of music owes to Spain. The country was for so long considered to be in a state of chronic political disturbance that few foreigners took up their abode there, except such as had business interests, and for the rest the mere traveller never became acquainted with the real life of the people, or entered into their intellectual amusements. It is quite a common thing to find the tourist entering in his valuable notes on a country which he has not the knowledge of the world to understand: " The Spaniards are not a musical people," and remaining quite satisfied with his own dictum. Yet Albert Soubies, in his *Histoire de la Musique*, says, in the volume devoted to Spain: " Spain is the country where, in modern times, musical art has been cultivated with the greatest distinction and originality. In particular, the school of religious music in Spain, thanks to Morales, Guerrero, and Victoria, will bear comparison with all that has been produced elsewhere of the highest and most cultivated description. The national

genius has also shown itself in another direction,
in works which, like the ancient *eglogas*—the contemporary *zarzuelas* of Lope de Vega and Calderon
—and the *torradillas* of the last century shine brilliantly by the verve, the gaiety, the strength, and
delicacy of their comic sentiment. . . . The
works of this class are happily inspired by popular art, which in this country abounds in characteristic elements. One notes how much the
rhythm and melody display native colour, charm,
and energy. In many cases, along with vestiges
of Basque or of Celtic origin, they show something of an Oriental character, due to the long
sojourn of the Moors in this country."

As regards this pre-eminence, it is enough to
remember that Spain was anciently one of the regions most thoroughly penetrated by Roman
civilisation. It is not too much to say that this
art has never sunk into decadence in Spain.
During the sixteenth century the archives of the
Pontifical chapel show the important place occupied by Spanish composers in the musical history
of the Vatican, and among the artists who gained
celebrity away from their own country were Esco-
ledo, Morales, Galvey, Tapia, and many others.
To the end of the seventeenth century a galaxy
of brilliant names carried on the national history
of Spanish music, both on religious and secular
lines; and though in the eighteenth and part of
the nineteenth centuries there was a passing invasion of French and Italian fashion, the true and

characteristic native music has never died out, and at the present time there is a notable musical renaissance in touch with the spirit and natural genius of the people.

A Royal Academy of Music has, within recent times, been added to the other institutions of a like kind, and native talent is being developed on native lines, not in imitations from countries wholly differing from them in national character- istics. Spaniards are exacting critics, and the best musicians of other countries are as well known and appreciated as their own composers and executants. Wagner is now a household word among them, where once Rossini was the object of fashionable admiration. The national and characteristic songs of Spain have been already referred to. They are perfectly distinct from those of any other nation. There is about them a dainty grace and pathos, combined fre- quently with a certain suspicion of sadness, which is full of charm, while those which are frankly gay are full of life, audacity, and "go," that carry away the listeners, even when the language is imperfectly understood. The charming songs, with accompaniment for piano or guitar, of the Master Yradier, are mostly written in the soft dialect of Andalucia, which lends itself to the music, and is liquid as the notes of a bird. The songs of Galicia are, in fact, the songs of Portu- gal; just as the Galician language is Portuguese, or a dialect of that language, which has less impress of the ancient Celt-Iberian and more of French than its sister, Castilian, both being descendants of Latin, enriched with words borrowed from the different nations which have at one time or another inhabited or conquered their country.

The guitar is, of course, the national instrument, and the songs never have the same charm with any other accompaniment; but the Spanish women of to-day are prouder of being able to play the piano or violin than of excelling in the instrument which suits them so much better. The Spaniard is nervously anxious not to appear, or to be, behind any other European nation in what we call " modernity," a word that signifies that to be " up-to-date " is of paramount importance, leaving wholly out of the question whether the change be for the better or infinitely towards the lower end of the scale.

The records of Spain in art, as in literature, are so grand, so European, in fact, that it is much if the artists of to-day come within measurable distance of those who have made the glory of their country. Nevertheless, the modern painters and sculptors of Spain hold their own with those of any country. After the temporary eclipse which followed the death of Velasquez, Ribera, and Murillo — the eighteenth century produced no great Spanish painter, if we except Goya, who left no pupils—Don José Madrazo, who studied at the same time as Ingres in the studio of David, began the modern renaissance. He became Court painter, and left many fine portraits; but, perhaps, as Comte Vasili says, "La meilleure œuvre de Don José fut son fils, Federico; de même que la meilleure de celui-ci est son fils Raimundo."

Raimundo Madrazo and Fortuny the elder, who married Cecilia Madrazo, Raimundo's sister, have always painted in Paris, and have become known to Europe almost as French artists. Fortuny, by his *mariage Espagnol*, became the head of the Spanish renaissance. Unfortunately, he has been widely imitated by artists of all nations, who have not a tithe of his genius, if any. Pradilla, F. Domingo, Gallegos, the three Beulluire brothers, Bilbao, Gimenez, Aranda, Carbonero, are only a few of the artists whose names are known to all art collectors, and who work in Spain. Villegas has settled in Rome. The exhibition of modern Spanish paintings in the London Guildhall last year (1901) was a revelation to many English people, even to artists, of the work that is being done at the present day by Spanish painters, both at home and in Paris and Rome. In sculpture, also, Spain can boast many artists of the highest class.

The drama in Spain has in all times occupied an important place. The traditions of the past names, such as Calderon, Lope de Vega, Tirso de Molina, Moreto, and others, cannot exactly be said to be kept up, for these are, most of them, of European fame; but in a country where the theatre is the beloved entertainment of all classes, and perhaps especially so of the poor or the working people, there are never wanting dramatists who satisfy the needs of their auditors, and whose works are sometimes translated into foreign languages, if not actually acted on an alien stage. It would be impossible and useless to give a mere list of the names of modern dramatists, but that of Ayala is perhaps best known abroad, and his work most nearly approaches to that of his great forerunners. His *Consuelo*, *El tejado de Vidrio*, and *Tanto por ciento* show great power and extraordinary observation. His style, too, is perfect. Señor Tamago, who persistently hides his name under the pseudonym of "Joaquin Estebanez," may also be ranked amongst the leaders of the modern Spanish drama, and his *Drama Nuevo* is a masterpiece. Echegaray belongs to the school of the old drama, whose characteristic is that virtue is always rewarded and vice punished. His plays are very popular because they touch an audience even to tears, and he has several followers or imitators. The comedies of manners and satirical plays are generally the work of Eusebio Blasco, Ramos Carrion, Echegaray the younger, Estremada, Alverez, though there are others whose names are legion. Echegaray is really a man of genius. A clever engineer and professor of mathematics, he was Minister of Finance during the early days of the Revolution. His first play took the world of Madrid by surprise and even by storm. *La*

Esposa del Vengador had an unprecedented success, and at least thirty subsequent dramas, in prose and in verse, have made this mathematician, engineer, and financier one of the most famous men of his day. His art and his methods are purely Spanish. I have already referred to the phenomenal success of Perez Galdós's *Electra* within the last few months. It must, however, be ascribed chiefly to the moment of its presentation rather than to any superlative merit in the drama. It is well written, which is what may be said of almost all Spanish plays, for the language is in itself so dignified and so beautiful that, if it be only pure and not disfigured by foreign slang, it is always sonorous and charming. To the state of the popular temper, however, and the coincidence of the political events already referred to must be ascribed the fact that a piece like *Electra* should cause the fall of a Government, and bring within dangerous distance the collapse of the monarchy itself. The excitement which it still produces, wherever played, is now in a great part due to the foolish action of some of the bishops and the fact that individual clerics use their pulpits to condemn it, and attempt to forbid its being read or seen.

Spain is not particularly rich in great actors, although she has always a goodly number who come up to a fair standard of excellence. The great actors of the day in Madrid are María Guerrero and Fernando Diaz de Mendoza. They obtained a perfect ovation during the last season in the play, *El loco Dios*, of Echegaray—a work which gives every opportunity for the display of first-class talent in both actors, and which led to a fury of enthusiasm for the popular dramatist, which must have recalled to him the early days of his great successes.

Since the beginning of the eighteenth century, Spain has had three great Academies, which, even in the troublous times of her history, have done good work in the domains of history, language, and the fine arts; but it is since the Revolution that they have become of real importance in the intellectual development of the nation, and other societies have been added for the encouragement of scientific research and music. The earliest of her academies was that of language, known as the Royal Spanish Academy. It is exactly on the lines of the Académie Française. Founded in 1713, its statutes were somewhat modified in 1847, and again in 1859. There are only thirty-six members, about eighty corresponding members in different provinces of Spain, and an unlimited, or at least undetermined, number of foreign and honorary correspondents. Besides the Central Society in Madrid, the Royal Spanish Academy has many corresponding branches in South America, such as the Columbian, the Equatorial, the Mexican, and those of Venezuela and San Salvador. The existence of academies of language in the South American States does not appear to effect much in the way of maintaining the purity of Castilian among them, for South American Spanish, as spoken at least, is not much more like the original language than the South American Spaniard is like the inhabitant of the mother country. The dictionary of the Royal Academy of Spain, like that of France, is not yet completed.

Philip V. founded the Royal Academy of History in 1738. Under its auspices, especially of late years, much valuable work has been done in publishing the original records of the country, to be found at Simancas and other places; but the authentic history of Spain is still incomplete. Up to the time of his assassination, Don Antonio Cánovas del Castillo was its director, and Don Pedro de Madrazo its permanent secretary. The society, now known as the Real Academia de San Fernando, founded in 1752, under the title of Real Academia de las tres nobles Artes, has now had a fourth added to it—that of music. The functions of its separate sections are much the same as those of the English Academy of Painting and the sister arts. A permanent gallery of the works of its members exists in Madrid, and certificates, diplomas, honourable mention, etc., are distributed by the directors to successful competitors.

Later societies are the Academies of Exact Science, Physical and Natural, of Moral and Political Science, of Jurisprudence and Legislation, and last, but by no means least, the Royal Acad-

emy of Medicine, under whose auspices medical
science has of late years made immense strides,
and is probably now in line with that of the most
advanced of other countries.

CHAPTER XVI

MODERN LITERATURE

THE name of Pascual de Gayangos is known
far beyond the confines of his own country
as a scholar, historian, philologist, biographer,
and critic. Although now a man of very advanced age, he is one of the most distinguished of
modern Orientalists, and his *History of the Arabs
in Spain*, *Vocabulary of the Arabic Words in
Spanish*, and his *Catalogue of Spanish MSS. in the
British Museum* are known wherever the language
is known or studied. He has published in Spanish an edition of Ticknor's great work on Spanish
literature, and has edited several valuable works
in the Spanish Old Text Society besides innumerable other historical and philological books and
papers, which have given him a European reputation. His immense store of knowledge, his
modesty, and his genuine kindness to all who
seek his aid endear him as much for his personal
qualities as for his learning.

Next to Gayangos in the same class of work,
Marcelino Menendez y Palayo may perhaps be
mentioned. His *History of Æsthetic Ideas in*

Spain has been left unfinished so far, owing to
the demands made on his time by his position in
the political world as one of the Conservative
leaders. Don Modesto Lafuente, though scarcely
possessing the qualities of a great historian, is accurate and painstaking to a great degree; but in
the field of history many workers are searching
the archives and documents in which the country
is so rich, and throwing light on particular periods.
Cánovas del Castillo, in spite of his great political
duties, was one of the most valuable of these; and
the eminent jurist, Don Francisco de Cardenas,
and the learned Jesuit, Fidel Fita, and other
members of the Academy of History are constantly working in the rich mine at Simancas.
New papers and books are continually being
brought out under the auspices of this society,
throwing light on the past history of the country.

Fernan Caballero, a German by race, but married successively to three Spanish husbands, may
be said to have inaugurated the modern Spanish
novel *de costumbres*, and her books are perhaps
better known in England than those of some of
the later novelists. By far the greater writer of
the day in Spain, however, in light literature, is
Juan Valera, at once poet, critic, essayist, and novelist. His *Pepita Jimenez* is a remarkable novel,
full of delicate characterisation and exquisite
style, second to none produced in any country—a
novel full of fire, and yet irreproachable in taste,
handling a difficult subject with the mastery of

genius. It has been translated into English; but however well it may have been done, it must lose immensely in the transition, because the Spanish of Valera is the perfection of a perfectly beautiful language. In this novel we have the character of a priest, who, while we know him only through the letters addressed to him by the young student of theology, the extremely sympathetic hero of the story, lives in one's memory, showing us the best side of the Spanish priest. Other novels of Valera's, *Doña Luis* and *El Comendador Mendoza*, a number of essays on all sorts of subjects, critical and other, and poems which show great grace and correctness of style, have given this writer a high place in the literature of the age.

Perez Galdós is a writer of a wholly different class, although he enjoys a very wide reputation in his own country and wherever Spanish is read. His *Episodes Nacionales*, some fifty-six in number, attract by their close attention to detail, which gives an air of actuality to the most diffuse of his stories. They are careful and very accurate studies of different episodes of national life, in which the author introduces, among the fictitious characters round whom the story moves, the real actors on the stage of history of the time. Thus Mendizábal, Espartero, Serrano, Narvaez, the Queen of Ferdinand VII., Cristina, and many other persons appear in the books, giving one the impression that history is alive, and not the record of long-dead actors we are accustomed to find it.

Galdós appears to despise any kind of plot; the events run on, as they did in fact run on, only there are one or two people who take part in them whom we may suppose to be creations of the author's brain. Certainly, one learns more contemporary history by reading these *Episodes* of Perez Galdós, and realises all the scenes of it much more vividly than one would ever do by the reading of ordinary records of events. As the tendency and the sympathy of the writer is always Liberal, one fancies that Galdós has written with the determined intention to tempt a class of readers to become acquainted with the recent history of their country who would never do so under any less attractive form than that of the novel. His works must do good, since they are very widely read, and are extremely accurate as history. His play, *Electra*, which is just now giving him such wide celebrity, is of the actual time, and the scene is laid wholly in Madrid. The freedom that he advocates for women is merely that which Englishwomen have always enjoyed, or, at least, since mediæval times, and has nothing in common with the emancipation which our " new women " claim for themselves. Galdós, also, is fond of introducing the simple-minded and honest, if not very cultivated, priest. His style is pure, without any great pretention to brilliancy, or any of the straining after effect which so many of the English writers seem to think gives distinction.

Pedro Alarcón is novelist first, and historian, poet, and critic afterwards. That is to say, his novels are his best-known and most widely read works. He has two distinct styles. His *Sombrero de Tres Picos* is a fascinating sketch of quaint old village life, full of quiet grace, while *El Escándalo* and *La Pródiga* are of the sensational order. He writes, like Galdós, in series, such as *Historietas Nacionales*, *Narraciones Inverosímiles*, and *Viajes por España*. Parada is a native of Santander, and writes of his beloved countrymen. *Sotilezas*, his best-known, and perhaps best, novel, treats of life among the fisher-folk of Santander, before it became an industrial town. Writing in dialect makes many of his stories puzzling, if not impossible for foreign readers.

The lady who writes under the pseudonym of "Emelia Pardo Bazan" may be said to be the leader or the pioneer of women's emancipation in the sense in which we use the words. She is a native of Galicia, and is imbued with that intense love of her native province which distinguishes the people of the mountains. Her novels are chiefly pictures of its scenery and the life of its people, though in at least one she does not hesitate to take her readers behind the scenes of student life in Madrid. It would not be fair to apply to this writer's work the standard by which we judge an English work, because in Spain there is a frankness, to call it by no other name, in discussing in mixed company subjects which it would not be thought good taste to mention under the same circumstances with us. *Una Cristiana* and *La Prueba*, its sequel, are founded on the sex problem, and, probably without any intention of offence, Pardo Bazan has worked with a very full brush and a free hand, if I may borrow the terms from a sister art. Her articles on intellectual and social questions show an amount of education and a breadth of view which place her among the best writers of her nation. She is not in the least blinded by her patriotism to the faults of her country, especially to the hitherto narrow education of its women. She holds up an ideal of a higher type—a woman who shall be man's intellectual companion, and his helper in the battle of life. She is by no means the only woman writer in Spain at the present time; but she is the most talented, and occupies certainly the highest place. Her writings are somewhat difficult for anyone not conversant with Portuguese, or, rather, with the Galician variety of the Spanish language, for the number of words not to be found in the Spanish dictionary interfere with the pleasure experienced by a foreigner, and even some Castilians, in reading her novels. Pardo Bazan was an enthusiastic friend and admirer of Castelar, and belongs to his political party. A united Iberian republic, with Gibraltar restored to Spain, is, or was, its programme.

Hermana San Sulpicio, by Armando Palacio Valdés, is one of the charming, purely Spanish novels which has made a name for its author beyond the confines of his own country; but since that was produced he has gone for his inspiration to the French naturalistic school, and, like some English writers, he thinks that repulsive and indecent incidents, powerfully drawn, add to the artistic value of his work. Padre Luis Coloma, a Jesuit, obtained a good deal of attention at one time by his *Pequeñeces*, studies, written in gall, of Madrid society. His stories are too narrowly bigoted in tone to have any lasting vogue, and his views of life too much coloured by his ultramontane tendencies to be even true. Nuñez de Arce is, like so many Spaniards of the last few decades, at once a poet and a politician. He played a stirring part from the time of the Revolution to the Restoration, always on the side of liberty, but never believing in the idea of a republic. His *Gritos del Combate* were the agonised expression of a fighter in his country's battle for freedom and for light. Since the more settled state of affairs, Nuñez de Arce has written many charming idyls and short poems. In the *Idilio* is a wonderful picture of the, to some of us, barren scenery of Castile, in which the eye of the artist sees, and makes his readers see, a beauty all the more striking because it is hidden from the ordinary gaze.

Of José Zorilla as a poet there is little need to speak. His countrymen read his voluminous works, but they are not of any real value. Cam-

poamor describes his *Dorloras* as " poetic compositions combining lightness, sentiment, and brevity
with philosophic importance." His earlier works
were studied from Shakespeare and from Byron,
who was the star of the age when Campoamor
began to write. His most ambitious work, the
Universal Drama, is " after Dante and Milton."
He is a great favourite with his fellow-countrymen, both as poet and companion. He is a member of the Academy and a Senator.

It is impossible, however, to do more than indicate a few of the writers who are leaders in the
literature of Spain to-day. There has, in fact,
been an immense impulse in the production of
books of all classes within the last twenty or
thirty years. In fiction, Spain once more aspires
to have a characteristic literature of her own, in
place of relying on translations from the French,
as was the case for a brief time before her political
renaissance began.

A notable departure has been the foundation
of the Folklore Society, and the publication up to
the present time of eleven volumes under the name
of *Biblioteca de las Tradiciones Populares Españolas*,
under the direction of Señor Don Antonio Ma-
chado y Alvarez. In the introduction to the first
volume, the Director tells us that, with the help
of the editor of *El Folklore Andaluz* and his
friends, D. Alejandro Guichot y Sierra and D.
Luis Montolo y Raustentrauch, he has undertaken this great work, which arose out of the

Bases del Folklore Español, published in 1881, and the two societies established in 1882, the Folklore Andaluz and Folklore Extremeño. These societies have for object the gathering together, copying, and publishing of the popular beliefs, proverbs, songs, stories, poems, the old customs and superstitions of all parts of the Peninsula, including Portugal, as indispensable materials for the knowledge and scientific reconstruction of Spanish culture. In this patriotic and historical work many writers have joined, each bringing his quota of garnered treasure-trove, presenting thus, in a series of handy little volumes, a most interesting collection of the ancient customs, beliefs, and, in fact, the folklore of a country exceptionally rich in widely differing nationalities.

Many of the tales, which it would seem even at the present time, especially in Portugal and Galicia, are told in the evening, and have rarely found their way into print, have the strong stamp of the legitimate Eastern fable, and bear a great family resemblance to those of the *Arabian Nights*. As, in fact, the *Thousand and One Nights* was very early published in Spanish, it is probable that its marvellous histories were known verbally to the people of the Iberian continent for many centuries, and have coloured much of its folklore. *The Ingenious Student* is certainly one of these. Barbers also play an important part in many of these tales. It is quite common for the Court barber to marry the King's daughter, and to succeed him as ruler; but the barber was, of course, surgeon or blood-letter as well as the principal news-agent—the forerunner of the daily newspaper of our times. The transmutation of human beings into mules, and *vice versa*, is a common fable, and we meet with wolf-children and the curious superstition that unbaptised people can penetrate into the domains of the enchanted Moors, and that these have no power to injure them. The story of the Black Slave, who eventually married the King's daughter and had a white mule for his Prime Minister, is very Eastern in character. " From so wise a King and so good a Queen the people derived great benefit; disputes never went beyond the ears of the Chief Minister, and, in the words of the immortal barber and poet of the city, ' the kingdom flourished under the guidance of a mule: which proves that there are qualities in the irrational beings which even wisest ministers would do well to imitate.' " *The Watchful Servant* is, however, purely Spanish in character, and it closes with the proverb that "a jealous man on horseback is first cousin to a flash of lightning." *King Robin*, the story of how the beasts and birds revenged themselves on Sigli and his father, the chief of a band of robbers, recalls " Uncle Remus " and his animal tales; for the monkeys, at the suggestion of the fox, and with the delighted consent of the birds and the bees, made a figure wholly of birdlime to represent a sleeping beggar, being quite certain that Sigli would kick it the moment that he saw the intruder from the windows of his father's castle. In effect both father and son became fast to the birdlime figure, when they were stung to death by ten thousand bees. Then King Robin ordered the wolves to dig the grave, into which the monkeys rolled the man and the boy and the birdlime figure, and, after covering it up, all the beasts and birds and insects took possession of the robbers' castle, and lived there under the beneficent rule of King Robin.

Silver Bells is, again, a story of a wholly different type, and charmingly pretty it is, with its new development of the wicked step-mother—in this case a mother who had married again and hated her little girl by the first husband. *Elvira, the Sainted Princess*, tells how the daughter of King Wamba, who had become a Christian unknown to her father, by her prayers and tears caused his staff to blossom in one night, after he had determined that unless this miracle were worked by the God of the Christians she and her lover should be burned.

One fault is to be found with these old stories as remembered and told by Mr. Sellers; that is, the introduction of modern ideas into the Old-World fables of a primitive race. Hits at the Jesuits, the Inquisition, and the government of recent kings take away much of the glamour of what is undoubtedly folklore. The story of the *Black Hand* seems to have many varieties. It is somewhat like our stories of Jack and the Bean

Stalk and Bluebeard, but differs, to the advantage
of the Spanish ideal, in that the enchanted prince
who is forced to play the part of the terrible Bluebeard during the day voluntarily enters upon a
second term of a hundred years' enchantment, so
as to free the wife whom he loves, and who goes
off safely with her two sisters and numerous other
decapitated beauties, restored to life by the self-
immolation of the prince. The *White Dove* is
another curious and pretty fable which has many
variations in different provinces—a story in which
the King's promise cannot be broken, though it
ties him to the hateful negress who has trans-
formed his promised wife into a dove, and has
usurped her place. Eventually, of course, the
pet dove changes into a lovely girl again, when
the King finds and draws out the pins which the
negress has stuck into her head, and the usurper
is "burnt" as punishment — an ending which
savours of the *Quemadero*.

The making of folklore is not, however, extinct
in Spain, a country where poetry seems to be an
inherent faculty. One is constantly reminded of
the Spanish proverb, *De poetas y de locos, todos
tenémos un poco* (We have each of us somewhat of
the poet and somewhat of the fool). No one can
tell whence the rhymed *jeux d'esprit* come; they
seem to spring spontaneously from the heart and
lips of the people. Children are constantly heard
singing *coplas* which are evidently of recent production, since they speak of recent events, and

17

yet which have the air of old folklore ballads, of concentrated bits of history.

> Rey inocente—a weak king,
> Reina traidora—treacherous queen,
> Pueblo cobarde—a coward people,
> Grandes sin honra—nobles without honour,

sums up and expresses in nine words the history of Goday's shameful bargain with Napoleon.

> En el Puente de Alcoléa
> La batalla ganó Prim,
> Y por eso la cantámos
> En las calles de Madrid.

> At the bridge of Alcoléa
> A great battle gained Prim,
> And for this we go a-singing
> In the streets of Madrid.

Señor Don Eugenio de Olavarria-y Huarte, in citing this *copla* (*Folklore de Madrid*), points out that it contains the very essence of folklore, since it gives a perfectly true account of the battle of Alcoléa. Although Prim was not present, he was the liberator, and without him the battle would never have been fought, nor the joy of liberty have been sung in the streets of the capital. There is seldom, if ever, any grossness in these spontaneous songs of the people—never indecency or double meaning. No sooner has an event happened than it finds its history recorded in some of these popular *coplas*, and sung by the children at their play.

The Folklore Society has some interesting information to give about the innumerable rhymed games which Spanish children, like our own, are so fond of playing, many of them having an origin lost in prehistoric times. One finds, also, from some of the old stories, that the devils are much hurt in their feelings by having tails and horns ascribed to them. As a matter of fact, they have neither, and cannot understand where mortals picked up the idea! The question is an interesting one. Where did we obtain this notion?

CHAPTER XVII

THE FUTURE OF SPAIN

A N Englishman who, from over thirty years' residence in Spain and close connection with the country, numbered among her people some of his most valued friends, thus speaks of the national characteristics:

"The Spanish and English characters are, indeed, in many points strangely alike. Spain ranks as one of the Latin nations, and the Republican orators of Spain are content to look to France for light and leading in all their political combinations; but a large mass of the nation, the bone and sinew of the country, the silent, toiling tillers of the soil, are not of this way of thinking. . . . There is a sturdy independence in the Spanish character, and an impatience of dictation that harmonises more nearly with the English character than with that of her Latin neighbours. . . . There is a gravity and reticence also in the Spaniard that is absent from his mercurial neighbour, and which is, indeed, much more akin to our cast of temper.

"True it is that our insular manners form at

first a bar to our intercourse with the Spaniard, who has been brought up in a school of deliberate and stately courtesy somewhat foreign to our business turn of mind; but how superficial this difference is may be seen by the strong attachment Englishmen form to the country and her people, when once the strangeness of first acquaintance has worn off; and those of us who know the country best will tell you that they have no truer or more faithful friends than those they have amongst her people."

Speaking of her labouring classes, and as a very large employer of labour in every part of the Peninsula he had the best possible means of judging, this writer says:

"The Spanish working man is really a most sober, hard-working being, not much given to dancing, and not at all to drinking. They are exceptionally clever and sharp, and learn any new trade with great facility. They are, as a rule, exceedingly honest—perfect gentlemen in their manners, and the lowest labourer has an *aplomb* and ease of manner which many a person in a much higher rank in this country might envy. When in masses they are the quietest and most tractable workmen it is possible to have to deal with. The peasant and working man, the real bone and sinew of the country, are as fine a race as one might wish to meet with—not free from defects—what race is?—but possessed of excellent sterling qualities, which only require knowing to be appreciated. I cannot say as much for the Government employees and politicians. Connection with politics seems to have a corrupt and debasing effect, which, although perhaps exaggerated in Spain, is, unfortunately, not by any means confined to that country only." [1]

In Spain to-day everything is dated from " La Gloriosa," the Revolution of 1868, the " Day of Spanish Liberty," as it well deserves to be called, and there is every reason to look back with pride upon that time; because, after the battle of Alcoléa, when the cry raised in the Puerta del Sol, *Viva Prim !* was answered by the troops shut up in the Government offices, and the people, swarming up the *rejas* and the balconies, fraternised with their brothers-in-arms, who had been intended, could they have been trusted by their commanders, to shoot them down, Madrid was for some days wholly in the hands of King Mob, and of King Mob armed. The victorious troops were still at some distance, the Queen and her *camarilla* had fled across the frontier, the Government had vanished, and the people were a law unto themselves. Yet not one single act of violence was committed; absolute peace and quietness, and perfect order prevailed. The ragged men in the street formed themselves into guards: just as they were, they took up their positions at

[1] *Commercial and Industrial Spain*, by George Higgin, Mem. Inst. C. E., London, 1886.

the abandoned Palace, at the national buildings and institutions; the troops were drawn up outside Madrid and its people were its guardians. Committees of emergency were formed; everything went on as if nothing unusual had happened, and not a single thing was touched or destroyed in the Palace, left wholly at the mercy of the sovereign people.   The excesses which took place in some of the towns, after the brutal assassination of Prim and the abdication of Amadeo, were rather the result of political intrigue and the working of interested demagogues on the passions of people misled and used as puppets.

With the advance of commerce and industry, and the massing of workers in the towns, has come, as in other countries, the harvest of the demagogue.   Strikes and labour riots now and then break out, and the Spanish anarchist is not unknown.   But the investment of their money in industrial and commercial enterprises, so largely increasing, is giving the people the best possible interest in avoiding disturbances of this, or of any other, kind: and as knowledge of more enlightened finance is penetrating to the working people themselves, the number who are likely to range themselves on the side of law and order is daily increasing.   The improved railway and steamer communication with parts of the country heretofore isolated, much of it only completed since this book was begun — in fact, within the last few months—is bringing the northern and western ports into prominence. Galicia now not only has an important industry in supplying fresh fish for Madrid, but has a good increasing trade with Europe and America. Pontevedra and Vigo, as well as Villagarcia, are improving daily since the railway reached them. Fresh fruit and vegetables find a ready market, and new uses for materials are coming daily to the front. Esparto, the coarse grass which grows almost everywhere in Spain, has long been an article of commerce, as well as the algaroba bean—said to be the locust bean, on which John the Baptist might have thriven—for it is the most fattening food for horses and cattle, and produces in them a singularly glossy and beautiful coat. This bean, which is as sweet as a dried date, is given, husk and all, to the mules and horses at all the little wayside *ventas*, and is now used in some of the patent foods for cattle widely known abroad. The stalk of the maize is used for making smokeless powder, and the husks for two kinds of glucose, two of cotton, three of gum, and two of oil. *Glucea dextrina* paste is used as a substitute for indiarubber. These products of the maize, other than its grain, are employed in the preparation of preserves, syrup, beer, jams, sweets, and drugs, and in the manufacture of paper, cardboard, mucilage, oils and lubricants, paints, and many other things. The imitation india-rubber promises to be the basis of a most important industry. Mixed with equal portions of natural gum, it has all the quali-

ties of india-rubber, and is twenty-four per cent.
less in cost.

A great deal has been said about the deprecia-
tion of the value of the peseta (franc) since the
outbreak of the war with America, but this unsatisfactory state of affairs is gradually mending;
and the attention of the Government is thoroughly
awakened to it. The law of May 17, 1898, and
the Royal decree of August 9 provide that if the
notes in circulation of the Bank of Spain exceed
fifteen hundred millions, gold must be guaranteed
to the half of the excess of circulation between
fifteen hundred and two thousand, not the half of
all the notes in circulation. The metal guarantee,
silver and gold, must cover half of the note circulation, when the latter is between fifteen hundred
and two thousand millions, and two-thirds when
the circulation exceeds two thousand. But the
Bank has not kept this precept, and there has, in
fact, been an illegal issue of notes to the value of
6,752,813 pesetas. So states the *Boletin de la
Cámara de Comercio de España en la Gran Bretáña*
of April 15, 1901.

The *Boletin*, after giving an account of the
English custom of using cheques against banking
accounts, instead of dealing in metal or paper
currency only, as in Spain, strongly advocates the
establishment of the English method. It is only
in quite recent years that there has been any
paper currency at all in Spain; the very notes of
the Bank of Spain were not current outside the

walls of Madrid, and had only a limited currency within.

Barcelona has long been called the Manchester of Spain, and in the days before the " Gloriosa " it presented a great contrast to all the other towns in the Peninsula. Its flourishing factories, its shipping, its general air of a prosperous business-centre was unique in Spain. This is no longer the case. Although the capital of Cataluña has made enormous strides, and would scarcely now be recognised by those who knew it before the Revolution, it has many rivals. Bilbao is already ahead of it in some respects, and other ports, already mentioned, are running it very close. Still, Barcelona is a beautiful city; its situation, its climate, its charming suburbs full of delightful country houses, its wealth of flowers, and its air of bustling industry, give a wholly different idea of Spain to that so often carried away by visitors to the dead and dying cities of which Spain has, unfortunately, too many.

It is becoming more common for young Spaniards to come to England to finish their education, or to acquire business habits, and the study of the English language is daily becoming more usual. In Spain, as already remarked, no one speaks of the language of the country as " Spanish "; it is always " Castellano," of which neither Valencian, Catalan, Galician, still less Basque, is a dialect—they are all more or less languages in themselves. But Castellano is spoken with a difference both by the *pueblo bajo* of Madrid and also in the provinces. The principal peculiarities are the omission of the *d—prado* becomes *praö*—in any case the pronunciation of *d*, except as an initial, is very soft, similar to our *th* in *thee*, but less accentuated. The final *d* is also omitted by illiterate speakers; *Usted* is pronounced *Uste*, and even *de* becomes *e*. *B* and *v* are interchangeable. One used to see, on the one-horsed omnibus which in old times represented the locomotion of Madrid, *Serbicio de omnibus* quite as often as *Servicio*. Over the *venta* of El Espirito Santo on the road to Alcalá—now an outskirt of Madrid—was written, *Aqui se veve bino y aguaardieñte*—meaning, *Aqui se bebe vino*, etc. (Here may be drunk wine).

The two letters are, in fact, almost interchangeable in sound, but the educated Spaniard never, of course, makes the illiterate mistake of transposing them in writing. The sound of *b* is much more liquid than in English, and to pronounce *Barcelona* as a Castilian pronounces it, we should spell it *Varcelona ;* the same with *Córdoba*, which to our ears sounds as if written *Córdova*; and so, in fact, we English spell it.

Spaniards, as a rule, speak English with an excellent accent, having all the sounds that the English possess, taking the three kingdoms, England, Scotland, and Ireland, into account.

Our *th*, which is unpronounceable to French, Italians, and Germans, however long they may have lived in England, comes naturally to the Spaniard, because in his own *d*, soft *c*, and *z* he has the sounds of our *th* in "*th*ee" and "*th*in." His *ch* is identical with ours, and his *j* and *x* are the same as the Irish and Scotch pronunciation of *ch* and *gh*.

The Spanish language is not difficult to learn—at any rate to read and understand—because there are absolutely no unnecessary letters, if we except the initial *h*, which is, or appears to us, silent—and the pronunciation is invariable. What a mine of literary treasure is opened to the reader by a knowledge of Spanish, no one who is ignorant of that majestic and poetic language can imagine. With the single exception of Longfellow's beautiful rendering of the *Coplas de Manrique*, which is absolutely literal, while preserving all the grace and dignity of the original, I know of no translation from the Spanish which gives the reader any real idea of the beauty of Spanish literature in the past ages, nor even of such works of to-day as those of Juan Valera and some others.

Picturesque and poetic ideas seem common to the Spaniard to-day, as ever. Only the other day, in discussing the monument to be erected to Alfonso XII. in Madrid, one of the newspapers reported the suggestion—finally adopted, I think—that it should be an equestrian statue of the young King, "with the look on his face with which he entered Madrid after ending the Carlist war." What a picture it summons to the imagination of

...ated by the ... readings of Mr. Foland, "The Wedding," and "The Letter from Ohio" being especially fine and demanding repeated encores. The 'cello solo was very highly appreciated as was Mr. soprano by Master Walsh. He has a wonderful soprano voice that took well with the audience.

The second half, "A Night in Venice," was especially fine. The program was arranged to give each member a part at his art and the selections met with much comment.

We now await the second number of the course with every assurance that it will be equally as fine.

CEMENT BLOCK BARN

Fairfield county. At the breaking up of the war in 1865 they came to Indiana and settled in Huntington county.

Twelve children were born to them, nine of which are living and three dying in infancy. Those living are, Amos F. Whitehurst of Kansas, Sarah J. Bilbee, of Mt. Zion, Ind., Mollie Abbott of Oklahoma, Chas. N. Whitehurst of Mt. Zion, Emma L. Duncan, Wabash, Ind., Angie Wiley, Texas City, Texas, Carrie Taylor, Warren, Ind., Jacob W. Whitehurst, Kansas, John Whitehurst, Wichita, Kansas.

She was converted while a young woman and joined the U. B. church in Ohio, but on moving to Indiana she joined the Christian church at Majenica and was a member of the church until the time of her death. She was a...

The Pastor and His Wife, Rev. and Mrs. W. W. Wiant

the boy King—for he was no more—in the pride
of his conquest of the elements of disorder and of
civil war, which had so long distracted his beloved
country—a successful soldier and a worthy King!

Spain is a country of surprises and of contradictions; even her own people seem unable to
predict what may happen on the morrow. Those
who knew her best had come to despair of her
emancipation at the very moment when Prim and
Topete actually carried the Revolution to a successful issue. Again, after the miserable fiasco
of the attempt at a republic, the world, even in
Spain itself, was taken by surprise by the peaceful restoration of Alfonso XII.

I can, perhaps, most fitly end this attempt at
showing the causes of Spain's decay and portray-
ing the present characteristics of this most interesting and romantic nation by a quotation from
the pen of one of her sons. Don Antonio Ferrer
del Rio, Librarian of the Ministry of Commerce,
Instruction, and Public Works, and member of
the Reales Academias de Buenas Letras of Seville
and Barcelona, thus writes, in his preface to his
Decadencia de España, published in Madrid in
1850: " It is my intention to point out the true
origin of the decadence of Spain. The imagination of the ordinary Spaniard has always been
captivated by, and none of them have failed to
sing the praises of, those times in which the sun
never set on the dominion of its kings." While
professing not to presume to dispute this former

glory, Señor Ferrer del Rio goes on to say that he only aspires to get at the truth of his country's subsequent decay. "There was one happy epoch in which Spain reached the summit of her greatness—that of the Reyes Católicos, Don Fernando V. and Doña Isabel I. Under their reign were united the sceptres of Castilla, Aragon, Navarra, and Granada; the feudal system disappeared—it had never extended far into the eastern limits of the kingdom—the abuses in the Church were in great measure reformed, the administration of the kingdom with the magnificent reign of justice began to be consolidated, in the Cortes the powerful voice of the people was heard; and almost at the same moment Christian Spain achieved the conquest of the Moors, against whom the different provinces had been struggling for eight centuries, and the immortal discovery of a new world. Up to this moment the prosperity of Spain was rising; from that hour her decadence began. With her liberty she lost everything, although for some time longer her military laurels covered from sight her real misfortunes." After referring to the defeat of the *Comuneros*, and the execution of Padilla and his companions, champions of the people's rights, he goes on to show that while the aristocracy had received a mortal blow in the reign of Ferdinand and Isabella in the cause of consolidating the kingdom and of internal order, they had retained sufficient power to trample on the liberties of the people, while they were not strong

enough to form a barrier against the encroach-
ments of the absolute monarchs who succeeded,
or to prevent the power eventually lapsing into
the hands of the Church. " Consequently, the-
ocracy gained the ascendency, formidably aided
and strengthened by the odious tribunal whose
installation shadowed even the glorious epoch of
Isabel and Fernando, absorbing all jurisdiction,
and interfering with all government. Religious
wars led naturally to European conflicts, to the
Spanish people being led to wage war against
heresy everywhere, and the nation—exhausted by
its foreign troubles, oppressed internally under
the tyranny of the Inquisition, which, usurping
the name of ' Holy,' had become the right hand
of the policy of Charles V., and the supreme
power in the Government of his grandson, Philip
II.—lost all the precious gifts of enlightenment
in a blind and frantic fanaticism. The people
only awoke from lethargy, and showed any ani-
mation, to rush in crowds to the *Autos da fé*, in
which the ministers of the altar turned Christian
charity into a bleeding corpse, and reproduced
the terrible scenes of the Roman amphitheatre.
Where the patricians had cried ' Christians to
the lions!' superstition shouted ' Heretics to the
stake!' Humanity was not less outraged than
in the spectacle of Golgotha. Spanish monarchs
even authorised by their presence those san-
guinary spectacles, while the nobles and great
personages in the kingdom thought themselves

honoured when they were made *alguiciles*, or familiars of the holy office. Theocratic power preponderated, and intellectual movement became paralysed, civilisation stagnated."

This has ever been the result of priestly rule. One can understand the feeling of the liberal-minded Spaniard of to-day that, without wishing to interfere with the charitable works inaugurated by the clergy, nor desiring in any way to show disrespect to the Church, or the religion which is dear to the hearts of the people, a serious danger lies, as the Press is daily pointing out, in the religious orders, more especially the Jesuits, obtaining a pernicious influence over the young, undermining by a system of secret inquisition the teachings of science, gaining power over the minds of the officers in the army, and establishing a press agency which shall become a danger to the constitution.

Spain's outlook seems brighter to-day than it has ever been since her Golden Age of Isabella and Ferdinand; and it is the people who have awakened, a people who have shown what power lies in them to raise their beloved country to the position which is her right among the nations of the world. But prophecy is vain in a country of which it has been said " that two and two never make four." This year, if all go well meantime, Alfonso XIII. will take the reins in his own hands —a mere boy, even younger than his father was when called to the throne; than whom, however,

Spain has never had a more worthy ruler. But Alfonso XII. had been schooled by adversity—he had to some extent roughed it amongst Austrian and English boys. He came fresh from Sandhurst and from the study of countries other than his own. To a naturally clever mind he had added the invaluable lesson of a knowledge of the world as seen by one of the crowd, not from the close precincts of a court and the elevation of a throne.

The child Alfonso XIII. has grown to be a man : a young man full of generous impulses, and deeply imbued by his wise mother in the duties and responsibilities of a constitutional monarch. To him, in the flower of his promising youth, Queen Christina has handed unimpaired the sceptre she bore so bravely in the anxious years of her son's long minority. Peace and a measure of prosperity have continued to smile upon Spain, and in the international councils of Europe the ancient monarchy bears an increasingly important part, in cordial friendship with the two great democratic forces, England and France. Those who on the memorable day in May, 1901, saw the King, so bright and eager, so manly yet so pathetically young, face his parliament and his people for the first time as their ruler, and with head erect and ringing voice swear to guard inviolate the Constitution by which he reigned, could not fail to be impressed with the earnest sincerity, the evident determination, of the young man to do right and fear nothing. Mistakes Alphonso XIII. may make, for he is human ; but it may be certainly predicted of him that, like his father before him, he will do no evil knowingly to his people ; and that he will, so far as in him lies, keep his pact with the subjects whose love and sympathy he has already gained.

The old politicians of the Revolution are dropping off one by one. Silvela, Sagasta, Romero-Robledo, and Pi y Margall have died since this book was written, and the newer statesmen who alternately govern Spain have found, as Canovas in his own words said of Alphonso XII., when he was of the same age as his son is now, that in Alphonso XIII. they "have a master." Like his father, too, the young King determined to marry for love, and to marry an English princess, bred in the free atmosphere of British life. When Alphonso XII. was urged by his ministers to adopt a measure limiting religious freedom in Spain, he replied : "There are two things upon which I will never give way, though it cost me my crown : I will never suppress religious liberty, and I will never marry against my will " ; and the influences whose activity in an opposite direction drew this declaration from Alphonso XII. have found in his son the same firm resolve to resist the retrogressive forces of bigotry, and to suffer no political coercion in the matter of his marriage. The Catholic faith is, and must remain, the religion of Spain ; but the day of religious persecution and tyrannical priestcraft is past for ever, and Catholic Spain is to be as free as Protestant England. The sympathies of Britons join those of Spaniards towards the young couple who under such hopeful auspices have begun life together. The national friendship typified by the personal union is a pledge of peace for Spain, and an advantage for England, and the closer communion between the peoples cannot but inspire Spain once more, as a similar friendship did well-nigh a century ago, with attachment to orderly liberty guaranteed by pure parliamentary government such as happily prevails in our own land.

For Spain most of the auguries are hopeful. The vexed question of "regionalism" in Biscay and Cataluna still stirs the nation to its heart; but the wisest of those who have hitherto clamoured for complete provincial autonomy are beginning to recognise that the best way of attaining the end they have in view is not to stand apart from the national life and cry for an impracticable separation, but for the wealthy, active provinces of the north to infuse into all departments of the national life some of their own energy and strength: for Biscay and Cataluna to conquer and influence the rest of Spain as Scotland has influenced the rest of Britain, and, whilst retaining in vigour provincial institutions, work for, and with, the nation as a whole. Whatever solution may be found for this and other burning questions, one thing may be foretold with confidence : The days of despotism have fled for ever from Spain. The law and not the crown shall rule ; and the bent of the young King, so far as it is known, encourages the hope that the popular liberties will have in time a strenuous champion and a faithful guardian. It must be the wish of all the English race, as it certainly is of Spaniards, that he with an English bride may reign long and happily over a free people ; and in the process of time be succeeded by Anglo-Spanish descendants handing down the traditions of popular government for future ages in a country which in the past despotism has done its best to ruin. Indeed, in the good sense of the Queen and her robust mind and body is the hope of the future of Spain.

PORTUGUESE LIFE
IN TOWN AND COUNTRY

CHAPTER XVIII

LAND AND PEOPLE

IT has been said, and it is often repeated, that if you strip a Spaniard of his virtues, the residuum will be a Portuguese. This cruel statement is rather the result of prejudice than arising from any foundation in fact. It has a superficial cleverness which attracts some people, and especially those who have but an imperfect knowledge of the true life and character of the people thus stigmatised.

Lord Londonderry, in Chapter VI. of his *Narrative of the Peninsular War*, writes thus of the difference of character between the two nations: "Having halted at Elvas during the night, we marched next morning soon after dawn; and, passing through a plain of considerable extent, crossed the Guadiana at Badajoz, the capital of

277

Estremadura. This movement introduced us at
once into Spain; and the contrast, both in personal appearance and in manners, between the
people of the two nations, which was instantly
presented to us, I shall not readily forget. Generally speaking, the natives of frontier districts
partake almost as much of the character of one
nation as of another. . . . It is not so on the
borders of Spain and Portugal. The peasant who
cultivates his little field, or tends his flock on the
right bank of the Guadiana, is, in all his habits
and notions, a different being from the peasant
who pursues similar occupations on its left bank;
the first is a genuine Portuguese, the last is a
genuine Spaniard . . . They cordially de-
test one another; insomuch that their common
wrongs and their common enmity to the French
were not sufficient, even at this time, to eradicate
the feeling.

"It was not, however, by the striking diversity
of private character alone which subsisted between
them, that we were made sensible, as soon as we
had passed the Guadiana, that a new nation was
before us. The Spaniards received us with a degree of indifference to which we had not hitherto
been accustomed. They were certainly not un-
civil. . . . Whatever we required they gave
us, in return for our money; but as to enthusiasm
or a desire to anticipate our wants, there was not
the shadow of an appearance of anything of the
kind about them. How different all this from

the poor Portuguese, who never failed to rend the air with their *vivats*, and were at all times full of promises and protestations, no matter how incapable they might be of fulfilling the one or authenticating the other!   The truth is that the Spaniard is a proud, independent, and grave personage; possessing many excellent qualities, but quite conscious of their existence, and not unapt to overrate them.   .   .   .   Yet with all this, there was much about the air and manner of the Spaniards to deserve and command our regard.   The Portuguese are a people that require rousing; they are indolent, lazy, and generally helpless. We may value these our faithful allies, and render them useful; but it is impossible highly to respect them.   In the Spanish character, on the contrary, there is mixed up a great deal of haughtiness, a sort of manly independence of spirit, which you cannot but admire, even though aware that it will render them by many degrees less amenable to your wishes than their neighbours.''

With due allowance for time and circumstances, much in this passage might have been written to-day instead of nearly ninety years ago, and one cause of the difference in feeling is no doubt explained truly enough.   Perhaps some shallow persons are affected by the fact that in good looks the Portuguese are as a race inferior to the Spaniards.   But there is no such real difference in character as to justify an impartial observer in using a phrase so essentially galling to England's

allies, of whom Napier said: "The bulk of the
people were, however, staunch in their country's
cause . . . ready at the call of honour, and sus-
ceptible of discipline, without any loss of energy."

Throughout the whole Iberian Peninsula the
main axiom of life appears to be the same:
"Never do to-day what you can put off to to-
morrow." On the left bank of the Guadiana it is
summarised by the word *mañana;* on the right
bank the word used is *amanhã.* There is only a
phonetic distinction between the Spanish and the
Portuguese idea. It is necessary for the traveller
in these countries to keep this axiom well in
mind, for it affords a clue to character and conduct the value of which cannot be over-estimated,
and not only to the character and conduct of individuals, but to the whole national life of the
inhabitants. In Portugal it permeates all public
and municipal life, and appears to affect most
especially that portion of the population who do
not earn their living by manual labour. The
higher one goes up the scale, the greater becomes
the evidence of the ingrained habits of dilatori-
ness and procrastination, and so any hard work
on the part of the lower class of toilers cannot be
properly directed, and the commerce and industry
of the country either dwindle away together, or
fall into the hands of more energetic and active
foreigners, who naturally carry off the profits
which should be properly applied to the welfare
and prosperity of the Lusitanians.

The mineral wealth and natural resources of the country are enormous, and it is really sad to contemplate the little use that is made of the one or of the other unless developed by alien energy and worked by alien capital. As regards this latter important factor, the administrative corruption and the unsound state of the national finances render it difficult to find foreign capitalists who are able and willing to embark in the industrial enterprises, the successful issue of which affords the only chance for this most interesting nation to recover something of its ancient prosperity and to once more take a position in the world worthy of the land of the hardy sailors and valiant captains who have left so imperishable a record over the earth's surface.

The intellectual life of Portugal seems to have ceased with Camoens. It is rather pathetic the way in which the ordinary educated Portuguese refers back to the great poet and to the heroic period which he commemorated. No conversation of any length can be carried on without a reference to Camoens and to Vasco da Gama. All history and all progress appear to have culminated and stopped then. Apparently nothing worthy of note has happened since. Camoens returned to Lisbon in 1569, and his great epic poem saw the light in 1572. He died in a public hospital in Lisbon in 1579 or 1580. In the latter year began the " sixty years' captivity," when Portugal became merely a Spanish province; yet there is no recollection of this — except the ingrained hatred of Spaniards and of everything Spanish—or of the shaking off the yoke in 1640, and of the battle of Amexial in 1663, where the English contingent bore the brunt of the battle, and the "Portugueses," as they are called by the author of *An Account of the Court of Portugal*, published in 1700, claimed the principal part of the honour. The traces of the Peninsular War have faded away, and on the lines of Torres Vedras there is scarcely any tradition of the cause of their existence. In Lisbon, indeed, there is one incident of later date than Camoens, which is considered worthy of remembrance,— the great earthquake of 1755,— but this can scarcely be looked upon as a national achievement, or a matter of intellectual development.

That Camoens is a fitting object for a nation's veneration cannot for a moment be doubted. The high encomium passed upon "the Student, the Soldier, the Traveller, the Patriot, the Poet, the mighty Man of Genius" by Burton, appears to be in no way exaggerated. The healthful influence of his life and writings has done and is still doing good in his beloved country. But though the man who in his lifetime was neglected, and who was allowed to die in the depths of poverty and misery, is now the most honoured of his countrymen, and his rank as one of the world's great poets is universally acknowledged, his labours have been to a certain extent in vain.

Not only industry, but culture, literature, and art appear to be infested with the mildew of decay. There is a good university at Coimbra, where alone, it is said, the language is spoken correctly. There is an excellent system of elementary and secondary schools, but in practice it is incomplete and subject to many abuses, like most public institutions in the country. The irregularities of the language, without authoritative spelling or pronunciation, and the best dictionary of which is Brazilian, have a bad effect upon the literature of the country.

The language, more purely Latin in its base than either of the other Latin tongues, with an admixture of Moorish, and strengthend by the admission of many words of foreign origin, introduced during the period of great commercial prosperity, possesses ample means for the expression of ideas and of shades of thought, and though it loses somewhat of the musical quality of the other languages in consequence of a rather large percentage of the nasal tones which are peculiar to it, yet it will hold its own well with the remaining members of the group.

Whatever the cause, however, there is hardly any general literature; almost the only books (not professional or technical) which are published, appear to be translations of French novels—not of the highest class. Perhaps in the study of archæology and folklore is to be found the most cultured phase of Portuguese intelligence. The Archæological Society of Lisbon strives to do good work, and has a museum with interesting relics in the old church of the Carmo, itself one of the most interesting and graceful ruins left out of the havoc caused by the great earthquake.

As might be expected under such circumstances, the newspapers are, with few exceptions, of the "rag" variety. Conducted for the most part by clever young fellows fresh from Coimbra, they are violent in their views and incorrect in their news, especially with regard to foreign intelligence. They have some influence, no doubt, but not so much as the same type of newspaper in France. The habitual want of veracity of the Portuguese character is naturally emphasised in the newspapers, and no one in his senses would believe any statement made in them.

A sure sign of the decadence of intellectual life, as well as of commercial activity, is to be found in the postal service, with its antiquated methods and imperfect arrangements. It is administered in a happy-go-lucky manner, which amuses at the same time that it annoys. Truly, with the post-office, it is well constantly to repeat to one's self the phrase: "Patience! all will be well to-morrow!" Probably it won't be well; but none but a foolish Englishman or Frenchman or German will bother about such a little matter.

A kindly, brave, docile, dishonest, patient, and courteous people, who, to quote Napier "retain a

sense of injury or insult with incredible tenac-
ity;'' and a due observance of their customs and
proper politeness are so readily met, and friendly
advances are so freely proffered, that a sojourn
amongst them is pleasant enough. I have won-
dered that the tourist has not found his way more
into this smiling land, though, no doubt, his
absence is a matter of congratulation to the traveller in these regions. The country has many
beauties, the people and their costumes are picturesque, and the cost of living—even allowing
for a considerable percentage of cheating—is not
excessive. There is, I suppose, a want of the
ordinary attractions for the pure tourist or globe-
trotter. There are churches, monuments, and
objects of interest in goodly numbers, and there
is beautiful scenery in great variety; but the true
attraction to a thoughtful visitor lies in the con-
templation of the people themselves.

The Portuguese, taken as a whole, are not a
good-looking race. The women, who, as a rule,
are very pretty as little girls, lose their good looks
as they grow up, and are disappointing when
compared with the Spaniards. Sometimes one
comes across fish- or market-women of considerable comeliness, which, when conjoined to the
graceful figure and poise induced by the habitual
carriage of heavy weights on the head and the
absence of shoes, makes a striking picture. The
costume is attractive, and the wealth of golden ear-
rings, charms, chains, and such like, in which these

women invest their savings, does not somehow seem anomalous or incongruous, though shown on a background of dirty and ragged clothing.

One unfortunate peculiarity that cannot help being noticed is the number of persons whose eyes are not on the same level. When this does not amount to an actual disfigurement, it is still a blemish which prevents many a young girl from being classed as a beauty. This and the peculiar notched or cleft teeth seem to point to an hereditary taint. Also unmistakable signs of a greater or lesser admixture of black blood are numerous. As a rule, the Portuguese are dark-complexioned, with large dark eyes and black hair; but, of course, one meets many exceptions. The men of the working class are fond of wearing enormous bushy whiskers, and women of all classes are accustomed to wear *moustachios*. The thin line of softest down which accentuates the ripe lips of the *senhorina* of some seventeen summers becomes an unattractive incident in the broad countenance of the stout lady of advancing years; and when, as sometimes happens, the hirsute appendages take the form of a thin, straggling beard, with a tooth-brush moustache, it can only be described as an unmitigated horror.

Society in Portugal is very mixed. There are the old *fidalgos*, haughty and unapproachable, and often very poor, the descendants of the nobles whose duplicity, ability in intrigue, and want of patriotism are so often alluded to in the pages of

Napier. Then there are the new nobility, the
"titled Brasileros," as Galenga calls them, who
have come back from Brazil to their native land
with large fortunes acquired somehow, and who
practically buy titles, as well as lands and houses.
Wealthy tradesmen, also, hold a special position
in the mixed middle class. There is, too, a
curious blending of old-fashioned courtesy with
democratic sentiments. The tradesman welcomes
his customers with effusive politeness—shakes
hands as he invites them to sit down, and chats
with these perhaps titled ladies without any affectation or assumption. After a while the parties
turn to business. A sort of Oriental bargaining
takes place, the seller asking twice as much as
the object is worth and he intends to take. The
purchaser meets this with an offer of about half
what she intends to give. With the utmost politeness and civility the negotiations are conducted
on either side. Each gives way little by little,
and in the end a bargain is struck. The amounts
involved appear to be enormous, as the *reis* are
computed by thousands and hundreds; but, then,
the *real* is only worth about the thousandth part
of three shillings and twopence at the present
rate of exchange, and the long and exciting
transaction, in all its various phases, has resulted
in one or other of the parties having scored or
missed a small victory. Verily, even to the loser,
the pleasure is cheap at the price.

The Brazilian element is most conspicuous in

Lisbon, and partly in consequence that city is only a little modern capital, somewhat feebly imitating Paris in certain ways, and, consequently, lacking the individuality and interest of Oporto. Yet Lisbon has a charm of its own; and the beauties of the Aveneida, the Roscio (known to the English as the " Rolling Motion Square," from its curious pattern of black and white pavement), the Black Horse Square, the broad and beautiful Tagus, the hills whereon the city is built, and the lovely gardens with their subtropical vegetation, will repay a stay of some weeks' duration.

Outside the mercantile element, there is considerable difficulty for a stranger to formulate the boundaries of other social strata. It would appear that the professions are in an indifferent position. Lawyers, of course, as in most other countries, are looked upon as rogues. How far this is the effect of the general prejudice, or whether it has any special foundation in fact, it would be hard to say. No doubt there are upright men amongst them, as in every other walk of life. There is a general idea that the medical training is lax, and the doctors, as a rule, are not highly considered. It is admitted, however, that they are as devoted, and as ready to risk their own lives, as those of other countries, a fact which was fully proved by several of the doctors at Oporto and Lisbon on the occasion of the outbreak of the plague in 1899.

The system of fees in general use tends to damage the position of both lawyers and doctors. In reply to the question as to his indebtedness, the client or the patient is told: " What you please." This sounds courteous, but is, in effect, embarrassing, as it is hard to estimate what is a fair fee under the circumstances, and generally one or the other of the parties is dissatisfied, and a sore feeling is left behind.

There are several orders of knighthood, which are showered about on occasion. The reasons for giving them are various. For instance, a Court tradesman may receive a decoration in lieu of immediate payment of a long-standing bill. The ribbons and buttons are not worn so freely as elsewhere on the Continent. The polite style in addressing a stranger is in the third person, and such titles as Your Excellency, Your Lordship, and Your Worship, sometimes enlarged with the adjective *illustrissimo* (most illustrious), are common enough. When an Englishman is first addressed as *Vossa Illustrissima Excellencia* (Your Most Illustrious Excellency), he begins to feel as if he were playing a part in one of Gilbert and Sullivan's comic operas. He soon gets used to it, however, and accepts the superlatives without turning a hair.

Of all classes it may be said that their manners are, on the whole, good, and their morals generally lax. Cleanliness has no special place assigned to it amongst the virtues. If it comes next to

19

godliness, then the latter must be very low down
the scale. It seems incredible, but verminous
heads are to be found in the ranks of well-to-do
tradespeople. Fleas and bugs abound, and happy
is he whose skin is too tough, or whose flesh is
too sour, to attract these ferocious insects. There
is not much luxury and there is a fair amount of
thrift, while frugality of living is common, especially among the populace.

One great characteristic is the intense love of
children which is exhibited by all classes, and
there is no surer way to the good will of a native
than a kindness, however slight, to a child in
whom he or she is interested. As is natural
under such circumstances, the children are shock-
ingly indulged and spoilt, with all the resultant
unpleasant and evil consequences. Cats, also,
are great favourites with the Portuguese, and the
thousands of shabby animals of Lisbon and Oporto
show no sign of fear if a stranger stops to stroke
them. They are accustomed to kind treatment,
and look upon all human beings as friends.

As a rule, a rather large number of servants are
employed. They are poorly paid, and in many
households indifferently fed and housed. Often
they are dirty, lazy, dishonest sluts. They chat-
ter shrilly with the master or mistress, answer and
argue when told of any shortcoming, and are
always ready to go off at a moment's notice. But
they are often capable of devoted service, and of
a sincere desire to be obliging, and may always

be counted on to exhibit the utmost kindness to the children of the house. Their written references, as a rule, are frauds. If you ask for the *boas referencias* (good references), so often mentioned in the advertisements of *criadas* (female servants), you will probably find that, even if genuine, they are antiquated, and that they leave many gaps between the various periods of service which can only be filled up by conjecture. *Criadas* are not, as a rule, of immaculate virtue, and give some trouble by their desire to go to *festas* and to servants' balls. The male servants are, as a rule, better than the *criadas*. Servants are somewhat roughly treated, and are ordered about as if they were dogs. It is always said that they do not understand or appreciate milder or more civil treatment, and are inclined to despise a master or mistress who uses the Portuguese equivalent to " please," or who acknowledges a service with thanks. I am inclined to doubt this, both from my personal observation and from a casual remark made to me by the landlady of a hotel at Cintra, that her waiters and servants much preferred English to native visitors, because of the greater politeness and consideration shown to them by the former. Of course, as in all other countries, servants are described as one of the greatest plagues in life; but this must be taken for what it is worth. And what would the ladies do without such a subject to grumble about ?

Portugal is a poor country, despite its natural

resources. The wealthy people are few, and consist mainly of returned Brazilians. It cannot be
said, either, that the classes in the enjoyment of
a competence constitute a fair average of the community. But the poor are very abundant. Wages
are terribly low, even a foreman in an engineering
shop getting only a milrei a day, averaging 3s.
2d. in English money. On the other hand, it must
be remembered that in such a climate the "living wage" is necessarily lower than in England.
Many necessities in England are superfluities or
even inconveniences under sunnier skies. The
people, too, are very frugal, and even in towns,
though rents be high, all other necessaries are
moderate in price. The standard of life is not
high, and the people are contented with a style
of living which would be indignantly rejected by
English labourers.

The artisans are not good workmen, but plod on
fairly well, and, with the exception of *festas*, require few holidays. They prefer to work on Sundays, and grumble at their English employers,
who generally split the difference, by closing their
shops for half a day. They look upon this as a
grievance, however much they may be assured
that it makes no difference in their wages.

A very hard-working class of men are the Gallegos, the natives of Galicia, who are nearly as
numerous in Lisbon as they were when Napier
wrote, and where, then as now, they act as porters,
messengers, scavengers, and water-carriers, and

are found in all sorts of lowly and laborious occupations. As porters and messengers, they have an excellent reputation for honesty, and for being most civil and obliging. Gallenga, a fairly shrewd observer, considers that the employment of these Spaniards has deplorable effects on the character of the Portuguese nation. I cannot go all the way with him in the gloomy view he takes of it, but it must be conceded that the existence of such a body of aliens (estimated at twelve thousand in Lisbon alone) working hard and well at occupations which the Portuguese will not do at all, or, if they attempt them, will do indifferently; herding together some ten or twelve in a small room, living on maize bread and a clove of garlic washed down with water; accepting thankfully a very attenuated hire, and yet contriving to send substantial savings back to Galicia,—must considerably affect the labour market and tend to keep wages low. They also close certain forms of labour to the native worker, and cause these industries to be looked on with contempt.

In towns like Lisbon and Oporto a great number of persons are employed in the fish trade. The fish-girls, with their distinctive costumes, their bare feet, and the graceful poise of the heavy basket of fish on their heads, are a very characteristic feature of both towns. The costumes differ in the two cities, mainly in the head-gear, but they are both picturesque and dirty, and emit the

same "ancient and fish-like smell." The men,
too, with their bare legs and feet, balancing a long
pole on the shoulder, with a basket of fish at each
end, will cover a marvellous amount of ground
in a day at the curious trotting pace which they
affect. Miles inland these men will carry their
finny wares, stopping at the public water-supplies
to moisten the cloth which protects the fish from
the sun and dust. These may or may not be fresh
when the day's work is nearly done, but housewives purchasing a supply in the afternoon had
better keep a very sharp look-out.

Fish plays an important part in the domestic
economy of dwellers within a reasonable distance
of the sea, and forms a considerable item in the
food-stuffs of the working classes. It is fairly
cheap, and is cooked so as to get the full value of
it. More important than the fresh fish is the
salted cod (*bacalhao*). This, which Napier described as "the ordinary food of the Portuguese,"
is the backbone of the worker's *menu*. It is not
fragrant, nor is it inviting in aspect in its raw
state, but it is said to be highly nutritive, and it
can certainly be cooked in ways which make it
appetising. The midday meal, which the wife
brings to her husband at his work, and shares
with him as they sit in the shade, is often composed of a *caldo* (soup) made of *bacalhao*, or of all
sorts of oddments, thickened with beans and
flavoured with garlic, accompanied by a bit of
rye-bread or of *broa*, the bread made from maize.

These soups and breads, accompanied by salads, onions, tomatoes, and other vegetables, washed down with draughts of a light red table-wine of little alcoholic strength, form the not unwholesome average diet of the worker with his hands. If he wants to get drunk, he can do so, with some difficulty, by imbibing sufficient wine, but the easiest method is to drink the fearful crude spirit *aguardente*. If he survive, he gets horribly, brutally drunk, and possibly does some mischief before he recovers. But it is only fair to say that he but rarely gets drunk, and that when he is thirsty he quenches his thirst with water, with a harmless decoction of herbs or lemonade, or with the almost innocuous wine. This sobriety is not the result of any temperance legislation or restrictions. No license is required for opening a shop for the sale of liquor. Only revenue dues and *octroi* duties have to be paid, and, of course, there is a liability to police supervision, which provides the police with a means of increasing their very inadequate pay by bribes or blackmail.

The amusements of the workman in the town are few enough, and mostly of a domestic character. He sits on his doorstep, or on a bench in the nearest gardens. He smokes the eternal cigarette, gossips with his neighbours, plays with his children, and pets the cat. His only real playtimes are the *festas*, when for some hours he indulges in revelry—if, indeed, it be worthy of such a title. He reads the newspaper but little,

—if he can read at all,—which is, perhaps, a good thing for him, and he is generally a Republican. This Republicanism is mostly academic, but the "red" type is not wanting, and a fiery spirit might be roused at any time, with consequences that cannot be foreseen. Of course, the younger men tinkle the guitar, and make love more or less openly to the girls. When age overtakes a man or misfortune overpowers him, there is no poor law to take him in charge, but there are extensive and well-organised charities in every centre which are eager and willing to assist those who are temporarily afflicted, and to afford sustenance—a bare sustenance, perhaps—to those who are permanently disabled.

The amusements of the town—the theatre, the concert, and the opera—do not affect the workman much; his budget does not allow of such indulgence, except on the occasion of a free performance. Though they are fairly musical and love the theatre, the Portuguese have no really æsthetic side to their character. There is a queer song and dance, topical and rather broad, the *chula*, the somewhat monotonous refrain of which is to be heard everywhere and at all hours, and from all manners of lips. The washerwomen kneeling by the brook bang the unfortunate clothes on the flat stones in rhythm with the tune, and beguile the time with the interminable song. It arises in unexpected places, and is a fairly sure item in the gathering of the younger folk, both in towns and villages, in the cool of the evening. Concerts and theatres are fairly patronised by the more moneyed classes, but the performances are not, as a rule, of a very high calibre. There is a subsidised theatre at Lisbon, but it does little to elevate the dramatic art elsewhere.

CHAPTER XIX

PORTUGUESE INSTITUTIONS

THE Portuguese army is raised by conscription, each parish, according to size, having to contribute an annual quota of young men between twenty and twenty-one years of age. These have to serve three consecutive years with the colours, and then pass into the reserve for another ten years. During the latter period no conscript can leave the country without a passport. In time of peace the army is supposed to number about thirty thousand men, and on the war footing should consist of about one hundred and twenty thousand men and two hundred and sixty-four guns. The men, who in summer wear brown holland clothes, look hardy enough, and, according to ordinary report, are worthy of the plucky *caçadores* of the Peninsular War, who, according to Napier, made most excellent soldiers when properly led. It is still said of the Portuguese soldier that with three beans in his pocket he can march and fight for a week without making any further demands upon the commissariat department. This military service does not affect the nation much, either morally or physically, and the only economical effect is probably that it provides a fruitful source of plunder to corrupt officials. As any man can free himself of the three years' service with the colours by paying a sum of about £24, it may be imagined what an opening this affords for special peculation.

The navy consists of about five thousand men, and of a few modern war-ships, and of some old boats whose seaworthiness is questionable. The best ship at present on the list is the cruiser *Dom Carlos*, which was sent to take part in the naval pageant which formed the first portion of the funeral of Queen Victoria. The sailors, who are much to be seen in Lisbon, where the great naval barracks are situated, look smart enough, and as the Portuguese have always been good sailors, it may safely be predicted that, in case of necessity, they will make the most of the limited means at their disposal, or of such of them as have not been utterly ruined by official indifference or worse.

In the towns one meets men in various employments, such as the police, who have served in the army, and still retain some sort of soldierly appearance, but once get into the country, and it is vain to look for any evidence of military service amongst the rural population.

The country-folk are a patient lot; most of them ruminants, like their own oxen. Sleepy always, and slow in their movements, they are often devoted to the farm, or *quinta*, on which they work, and are, perhaps, slightly more honest than their fellows in the towns. They are frugal enough, and enjoy their huge junks of dark bread, washed down with water, at their midday meal, and a sound sleep under the shade of an orange tree or a eucalyptus, or a bit of a wall, until it is necessary to begin work again. The peasant costumes are not inviting; they are simply squalid. Costumes in the towns are much better. Still, on festal days the village women deck themselves out with bright-hued shawls, and the men wind brighter scarfs round their waists to keep up their patchwork trousers, and thus relieve what would otherwise be the intolerable dinginess of the whole scene. The farmer himself, mounted on his mule, with high-peaked saddle and enormous wooden stirrups decorated with brass, his cloak, with the bright scarlet or blue lining folded outwards, strapped on in front, with his short jacket and broad-brimmed hat, offers a smart and typical figure.

In town or country, the beautiful oxen are worthy of admiration. They are the most satisfactory of all the rural animals. Horses, shabby and attenuated, little sheep of a colour from black to dirty grey, showing affinity to goats, and having neither the grace of the latter nor the sleepy comeliness of our own sheep, black and white cows whose points would not be much thought of by judges at an agricultural show, goats of all

sorts of breeds, and finally pigs of a most lanky
and uninviting appearance, form the stock of the
farms.   Heaps of chickens of all sorts run about
everywhere, and enjoy fine dust-baths by the side
of the road.

The aspect of the country varies much between
north and south.   In the former, one sees real
grass and hedges, and the bright flowers that are
common everywhere look all the better for their
green background.   The commonest hedge in the
south, and occasionally in the north, is made of a
few layers of stones loosely laid together with
a row of aloe plants on the top.   These grow
formidable in time, with huge sharp-pointed
leaves, and they present a curious appearance
when at intervals in such a row plants send up
their huge flowering stems from nine to twelve
feet high, looking at a little distance like telegraph poles.

Despite the squalid clothes of the peasants,
there are many picturesque aspects of rural life.
The driving of large herds of cattle by mounted
men, armed with long goads, is an interesting as
well as an artistic sight, and the same may be said
of the primitive agricultural occupations.   The
crops are harvested with a sickle, and you may
wake up some morning to see the field opposite
your house invaded by some twenty to thirty
reapers, men and women, boys and girls, patiently
sawing their way through the wheat or barley, or
whatever it is.   The corn is threshed out with the

flail, or trodden out by the oxen—all operations fair to look upon.   Forms of cultivation interesting to watch are the very primitive ploughing, the hoeing of the maize, and all those connected with the culture of the vines and the orange and other fruit trees, and especially the irrigation, which is so important to these latter.   In fact, one of the most charming of rural sights is the old water-wheel, groaning and creaking as it is turned by the patient ox or mule or pony, splashing the cool water from the well out of its earthen pots—each with a hole in the bottom—and discharging it into the trough leading to the irrigation channels or to the reservoir from which the water may afterwards be let off in the required direction.

But agriculture is not always so backward and primitive.   There are great landowners and large farmers who use the newest and best agricultural implements.   The Government does what it can to encourage the use of artificial manures, and there are societies which render important services to agriculturists and to fruit-growers.   Amid such labours live the quiet country-folk.   They have no thought of anything; they have no special amusements beyond an occasional *festa* and a dance.   They sit round the village well in the evening, and when not talking scandal, tell stories about—" Once upon a time there was a poor widow with one or more daughters," or " There was once a king's son "—often a Moorish king.

The old well-known tales reappear, modified to the Portuguese character and morality.

The following is a story taken from Braga's excellent book: "There was, once upon a time, a poor widow that had only one daughter. This girl, going out to bathe in the river with her companions on St. John's eve, at the advice of one of her friends, placed her ear-rings on the top of a stone, lest she should lose them in the water. While she was playing about in the river an old man passed along, who, seeing the ear-rings, took them and placed them in a leather bag he was carrying. The poor child was much grieved at this, and ran after the old man, who consented to restore her belongings if she would search for them inside his sack. This the girl did, and forthwith the artful old man closed the mouth of the bag and carried her off therein. He subsequently told her that she must help him to gain a living, and that whenever he recited—

> 'Sing, sack,
> Else thou wilt be beaten with a stick!'

she was to sing lustily. Wherever they came he placed his sack on the ground, and addressed the above formula to it, when the poor girl sang as loud as she could:

> 'I am placed in this sack,
> Where my life I shall lose,
> For love of my ear-rings,
> Which I left in the stream.'

The old man obtained much money from the audiences attracted by his singing leather bag. The authorities of one town, however, became suspicious, and, examining the sack while its owner was asleep, found and released the child. They filled up the bag with all the filth they could pick up, and left it where they had found it. The little girl was sent back to her mother. When the old man woke next morning, and took out the sack to earn his breakfast, the usual incantation had no effect, and when he applied the threatened stick the bag burst, and all the filth came out, which he was compelled to lick up by the enraged populace." At the close of the story the cigarettes glow, the white teeth gleam, the bushy whiskers wag, the old women chuckle, the girls giggle, and the youths snigger, and as the short twilight is now over, the group breaks up, and each vanishes into his or her own vermin-pasture to sleep until *amanhã* has actually become to-day, and the sun shines on another exact repetition of yesterday.

The Portuguese are superstitious, and are devout up to a certain point, and the clerics are exceedingly intolerant. In the morning one sees, as in all Roman Catholic countries, devout worshippers kneeling about in the churches before their favourite shrines, but, unlike the practice of most Roman Catholic countries, the churches are closed at or about noon for the most part, and are only open for special masses after that time. The procession of the Host is greeted with most extreme reverence, and whether it be in the fashionable Chiado at Lisbon or along a country lane, all uncover and make the sign of the cross, and many, even fashionably dressed ladies and gentlemen, kneel down and bow themselves humbly as the sacred wafer passes by, borne by the gorgeously vested priest; at least, in the cities the vestments are gorgeous, and a long train of acolytes and attendants makes the procession imposing, but in the country the vestments are often mildewed and decayed, and the one or two rustic attendants are not dignified in appearance. Still, the sacred symbol is the same, and the reverence and the devotion are the same.

There is an excessive hierarchy for the size of the country, there being in Portugal proper three ecclesiastical provinces, ruled respectively by the Patriarch of Lisbon and by the Archbishops of Braga and Evora. Besides these, there is the colonial province which is ruled by the Archbishop of Goa. Archpriests and other dignitaries abound, so that a priest has something to look forward to in the way of promotion; and yet, as a rule, the priests perform their duties without zeal and in a slovenly manner. One often hears it said that their behaviour and their morality leave much to be desired. There are among them gentlemen of blameless life and even of ascetic practices, but it is commonly reported that, as a whole, they are of inferior birth and education. It is not easy for a stranger to form any opinion on these points, but it must be conceded that their appearance is generally suggestive of the truth of the statement, and it may be admitted that there is an undue proportion of ignoble and sensuous faces amongst them.

Funerals are occasions of great pomp, and are often picturesque enough, while the masses for the dead at intervals after and on the anniversary are, no doubt, profitable to the Church. By attending these one has a good opportunity of testifying to the esteem in which the deceased was held, or to one's good will towards the family or representatives. These masses are generally advertised in the papers, with thanks to those friends who have attended funeral masses. As there is scarcely any intellectual activity in Portugal, there is practically no religious thought. A dull acquiescence in the dictates of the Church may be crossed by an occasional gleam of rebellion against sacerdotalism, roused by some temporary stirring up of the hatred felt against the Jesuits. But it in no way alters the habitual attitude of the people towards religion and its outward manifestations. One thing is certain, and that is that in town or country a man or a woman must be in the lowest depths of poverty and distress to refuse to throw a few *reis* into the bags of the licensed mendicants who, bareheaded, and clad in scarlet or white gowns, go round soliciting alms for the support of the churches on whose behalf they are sent out.

As is customary in most countries, the women are more amenable to religious influences than the men, and are more under the dominion of the priest. This is not likely to be altered yet awhile, for, under the present system of education and bringing up, the female portion of the community is not only not intellectual, but may even be described as being unintelligent. They are slovenly, and cannot be described as good housewives. They are pleasure-loving and garrulous, though this latter trait is not, I suppose, a specially national characteristic. They do much hard work, especially in the fields. In the classes above (if *above* be the proper word) the hand-workers, the young girls are still kept very strictly, and are not allowed to go out alone. Their knowledge of life is limited to the view from the windows of their homes, where they may be seen looking out on the street scenes below whenever the shade allows them to stand at the window or on the balcony. No " new woman " movement of any importance has yet taken place, and though there are modifications in woman's position in the national life, it is probable that it will take one if not more generations before women in Portugal achieve the emancipation which their sisters have attained in more progressive countries.

In one circumstance, however, woman does take her place by the side of man, and that is in the bull-ring—not, indeed, in the arena, but in every part of the amphitheatre, from the worst seats on the sunny side to the costly boxes in the shade. She takes as great an interest in the bull-fight as the man, and if she does not shout and swear, or fling her hat into the ring in her enthusiasm, she delights probably more than the man in the beauty of the spectacle, and appreciates almost as fully the feats of skill and daring which give such special attraction to the national pastime. This is a right royal sport, and as in Portugal the horrid cruelty which defaces it in Spain is absent, there is no overwhelming reason why the women should not sit and applaud the picturesque scene and the exhibitions of pluck and agility shown by the performers.

The scene is really magnificent, and the enthusiasm of the audience must be witnessed in order to understand the underlying potentialities of the Portuguese character. The vile abuse of a bull who will not show fight is comical to listen to. Probably, in such a case, the bull has been through it all before, and he does not care to make wild rushes at cloaks which have nothing substantial behind them. So he paws up the sand and looks theatrical, but refuses to budge. Then a nimble *bandarilhero* faces him, and fixes a pair of *bandarilhas* in his neck—one on each side if he can manage it. This is unpleasant, no doubt, but the bull's former experience tells him that it is not serious, and not even very painful. It was irritating the first time, but no well-bred

bull should condescend to be upset by such a
trifle. Another pair of *bandarilhas*, and yet
another, are fixed into his shoulders by their
barbed points—or the attempt is made to fix
them. Then the bull begins to play the game in
a condescending sort of way. Then the great
man, the *espada* himself, comes on the scene, and
arranges and waves his scarlet flag, and walks up
to the obstinate animal, perhaps flicks him in the
nostrils with his pocket-handkerchief and calls
him *vacca* (cow)! At last, seemingly out of good
nature, the bull rushes at the red flag, has the
highly decorated dart stuck between his shoulders,
by the daring *espada* who may perform some other
feat, listens to the applause, and laughs to himself
when he hears the bugle-call and sees the trained
oxen rush in with their long bells and their at-
tendant herdsmen, and with more or less of a
frolicsome air he trots out of the arena in their company and, having had his sore shoulders attended
to, and having had a good feed, chews the cud
with a pleasant reminiscence of the afternoon's
work. It is a mistake not to kill the bull, which
is not cruel in itself, but which would prevent
some rather tiresome interludes when a knowing
old bull refuses to be coaxed into playing his part
of the game.

Far different, however, is the scene when a
really spirited bull comes in with a rush and
charges wildly at the brightly attired performers,
and makes them skip over the barrier, often

leaving their cloaks behind them. Sometimes the bull skips over too, and then there is a most amusing scene, as performers, attendants, and all vault back over the barrier into the ring itself. When the *espada* finally performs his courageous feat under such conditions, he obtains such an ovation as his skill deserves. Hats of all sorts and shapes are cast to him in the arena, which he has to pick up and throw or hand back to the admirers who testify their satisfaction in this curious manner. Cigars, also, are thrown at the successful bull-fighter's feet, and these he keeps. The most famous *espadas* are all Spaniards, and they all wear the traditional dress of their calling. If, on the one hand, there is not the thrill of the actual killing of the bull, on the other there are no miserable old horses to be ripped up, and no smell of blood. Next to the actual bull-fights come the selections of the young bulls from the herds, when the members of the Tauromachian Societies exhibit their skill, and where many a gay young fellow gets much knocked about in exhibiting his agility or the want of it.

Other sports cannot be said to have any marked existence. Dancing is a national amusement, and a few of the Anglicised Portuguese go in for cricket and lawn-tennis. Cycling, though not unknown, is far from common, the roads being, as a rule, much too bad for comfortable or even for safe riding.

Local and provincial government leaves much

to be desired in Portugal. The keeping up of the roads is inconceivably bad. A royal road (*estrada real*) is generally the worst of all, and, with such an example before them, it is not to be wondered at that local authorities neglect their duties in this matter.

" No capital city in Europe suffers so much as Lisbon from the want of good police regulations." This quotation from Napier might very well be written to-day, and extended to include all Portuguese towns. Perhaps it is fair to say that it is not so much the regulations that are at fault as the incompetence and indifference of each local authority, which irresistibly suggest that corruption alone can account for such a mass of evil. The administrative machine is elaborate, and ought to be more effective. First, there is the district, ruled by the Civil Governor, an officer somewhat resembling a French prefect, with its corporate body known as the District Commission. There are seventeen districts, which are subdivided into two hundred and sixty-two communes. The head of a commune is the Administrator, and the corporation is known as the Municipal Chamber. The last subdivision is that of the communes into parishes, of which there are three thousand seven hundred and thirty-five. Each of these has as its head an officer called a *regedor*, and occupies the attention of *a junta de parochia*, or parish council.

The scavenging, sanitation, watering, paving,

and all the other works which fall within the
sphere of the municipality or local authority are
defective and neglected. The one bright point,
both in Oporto and Lisbon, is the care, skill, and
attention with which the public gardens and
squares are tended. The palms, tree-ferns, cacti,
and other semi-tropical and sub-tropical plants
are beautiful in themselves, and are arranged and
intermingled with other trees and shrubs in a
most artistic manner. The grass (upon which no
one, of course, may walk) is kept green by constant watering, and affords a delightful contrast
to the generally dry and dusty aspect of the city.
Another organisation which is generally efficient
and well conducted is that of the fire brigades.
The municipal firemen—the *bombeiros*—are often
stimulated by a healthy rivalry with the volun-
teer brigades, which are numerous, well found,
and, as a rule, well managed. The latter are
often centres of good charitable work outside
their actual fire service, and they are valuable
as offering a fair and worthy opportunity for the
display of sound public spirit and good feeling.

Though Portuguese laws are, as a rule, admirable in themselves, the administration thereof is
bad in the extreme, and the judiciary have a
reputation for turpitude remarkable even amongst
the recognised corruption of all officials. In Portugal proper there are two judicial districts—that
of Lisbon and that of Oporto. Each has a high
court known as a *Relação*, and there are inferior

courts of various styles and titles. Above all is
the Supreme Tribunal of Justice at Lisbon, which
is the final court of appeal, and the reputation of
which is somewhat better than that of any other
tribunal. The administration of criminal justice
is naturally amongst the worst. According to
common repute, the only consideration with the
judges is how they are to get the costs paid—
whether they are more likely to obtain them
through an acquittal, which throws them on the
prosecutor, or by a conviction. Also, it is generally said that the police themselves are recruited
from amongst the very lowest classes.

The prisons are described as being something
awful, only to be equalled in Morocco and savage
countries. In the market-place of beautiful Cintra
stands the prison, against the barred windows of
which crowd the prisoners, begging for money,
cigarettes, and food, which are supplied to them
through the prison bars by their friends and sym-
pathisers, and by soft-hearted people. Those
who are incarcerated in the upper story have
baskets, which they lower by means of strings,
so that they may be supplied in the same manner.
This seems to have amused Miss Leck (*Iberian
Sketches*, Chap. VI.), but it assumes a much more
serious aspect when one considers that in those
filthy dens all the prisoners are huddled together
—old men and boys, the murderer and the petty
thief, habitual criminals and unfortunate persons
taken into custody on mere suspicion, or charged

with an alleged breach of some police or even railway regulation; for it must be remembered that a station-master has nearly the same power as a policeman in taking a person into custody. "No one shall be put in prison," says the Portuguese code, "except under special circumstances"; but when the exceptions are considered, they are found to cover nearly every abuse of authority on the part of the pettiest official which can be conceived. Hence, all persons are obliged to submit to gross injustice and to a certain amount of blackmail if they wish to avoid the noisome experiences of a Portuguese gaol.

The Portuguese must be undoubtedly "of a docile and orderly disposition," as Napier says, or the crying injustices to which they submit with such patience would lead them to revolt; and if this were to happen, who could attempt to predict what excesses would be left uncommitted by a violent southron mob whose passions had been roused to such a pitch of activity? Perhaps *paciencia* and *amanhã* have their utility, and enable the people to bear the ills they have. They can even joke and caricature themselves, and though the comic journals are neither brilliant nor artistic, they show, at least, that a sense of humour is still left in our Lusitanian friends.

INDEX

PORTUGUESE LIFE

Index 325

THE END